INVEST EARLY, LIVE FREE

SIMPLE MONEY LESSONS FOR LONG-TERM WEALTH AND FINANCIAL FREEDOM

BISWAJIT MODAK

Made with ♥ on the Notion Press Platform
www.notionpress.com

Contents

Contents

Acknowledgements

This book exists because of quiet influences rather than loud inspiration.

I am grateful to the people and experiences that shaped my understanding of money long before this book was written — through observation, mistakes, patience, and reflection.

To those who taught me, directly or indirectly, that financial decisions are shaped less by intelligence than by behaviour — thank you. To the many ordinary people whose real-life struggles, questions, and discipline influenced the thinking behind these pages — this book carries your lessons.

I also acknowledge the value of time, consistency, and restraint — principles that rarely attract attention but quietly build stability. This book is rooted in those ideas.

Special thanks to my colleague, Iftikar Jahid, whose guidance, encouragement, and support helped bring this book to publication.

Finally, I thank every reader who chooses to slow down, think clearly, and take responsibility for their financial journey. If this book helps even a few people make calmer, more intentional decisions, its purpose will be fulfilled.

Preface

This book was not written to impress you. It was written to protect you.

Financial mistakes rarely appear dramatic at first. They accumulate quietly over time.

Most people do not fail with money because they are careless. They fail because no one ever explained money in a calm, honest, and practical way.

From childhood, we are taught to earn. Rarely are we taught how to **keep**, **protect**, and **grow** what we earn.

As a result, many intelligent, hardworking people:

- Save diligently but begin investing too late
- Buy financial products they do not fully understand
- Break long-term investments during emergencies
- Carry loans that quietly delay their financial freedom

These mistakes are not caused by a lack of effort. They are caused by a lack of clear guidance.

This book exists to interrupt that cycle.

If you are holding this book, you already care about managing money wisely — and that puts you ahead of most people who never pause to reflect on their financial decisions.

You will not find shortcuts here. You will not find stock tips, guarantees, or hype.

This book does not promise quick wins, overnight wealth, or effortless success. Instead, it focuses on decisions that quietly protect your financial future when life becomes uncertain.

What you will find instead is:

- Clear thinking instead of complex jargon
- Behavioural clarity instead of product obsession
- Practical systems that work quietly over decades

This is a book for people who want **financial peace**, not financial noise. For people who value stability over excitement. For people who understand that wealth is built slowly — and protected deliberately.

You do not need to read this book quickly, and you do not need to agree with every idea immediately.

Read it thoughtfully. Apply it patiently. Let time do the rest.

The first chapter begins with one of the most common misunderstandings about money — the belief that saving alone is enough.

If even a few financial decisions in your life become calmer, wiser, and more intentional because of these pages, then this book has done its job.

In personal finance, a few good decisions repeated over time can change an entire future.

Understanding Money the Modern Way

Fix your money mindset before investing even one rupee.

CHAPTER ONE

Why Saving Money Is Not Enough Today

A quiet problem most people don't notice

Most people believe they are doing the right thing with money. They earn, pay bills, save a little, and feel responsible. Saving gives a sense of safety. But in today's world, **saving alone is often not enough**.

The problem is not laziness or a lack of income. The real problem is that **the cost of living keeps rising quietly**, while most savings grow very slowly. Over time, this gap can reduce choices in life — education plans get delayed, medical emergencies feel heavier, and retirement becomes stressful instead of peaceful.

This chapter explains *why* this happens and *what simple mindset shift* can protect your future.

How rising prices slowly weaken savings (Indian reality)

In everyday life, prices do not stay the same over time. Food, fuel, rent, school fees, and healthcare usually become more expensive with time. This increase is called **inflation**.

Here are **real-life Indian-style examples** (illustrative, rounded figures):

Expense	Around 2010	Around 2026	Increase
Rice (1 kg)	₹22	₹55	~150%
Petrol (1 litre)	₹52	₹110+	~110%
School fees (monthly)	₹800	₹3,500	~330%
Doctor consultation	₹150	₹600	~300%
Rent (2BHK, small town)	₹4,000	₹10,000	~150%

Everything costs more over time

When prices rise like this, money kept in low-interest savings accounts slowly loses its buying power.

He Did Everything Right — And Still Felt Behind

In 2012, Amit was 26 and proud of his first job. His starting salary was modest, but he was disciplined. Every month, he saved ₹5,000 in his bank account before spending on anything else.

His friends spent on gadgets and trips. Amit did not.

He believed he was being smart.

By 2024, he had saved nearly ₹10 lakh. Seeing that number gave him confidence. He felt secure. Responsible. Ahead of others.

Then life moved faster than his savings.

His rent had doubled. Petrol crossed ₹110 per litre. His daughter's school fees were far higher than he imagined. A medical emergency for his father forced him to withdraw a large part of his savings.

For the first time, he felt something unexpected — not pride, but pressure.

He had not wasted money. He had not taken reckless risks. He had not been careless.

Yet he felt financially weaker than before.

The number in his bank account had grown. But its power had quietly shrunk.

That was the year Amit understood a truth no one had explained to him when he started working:

Saving alone is not enough in a world where everything becomes more expensive.

He didn't lose money. He lost time.

And in personal finance, time is the one thing you can never earn back.

Amit's mistake was not laziness. It was incomplete financial knowledge.

What inflation really means (in simple words)

Inflation means **the same amount of money buys less in the future.**

If inflation averages around 6% per year, then:

Time	Value of ₹1,00,000
Today	₹1,00,000
After 5 years	~₹74,000
After 10 years	~₹55,000

Inflation quietly reduces purchasing power

Even though the number in your bank may look the same, its real value decreases.

Saving vs. investing — not the same thing

Saving and investing serve **different purposes.**

Aspect	Saving	Investing
Main purpose	Safety & access	Long-term growth
Risk level	Very low	Controlled / managed
Time horizon	Short-term	Long-term
Beats inflation?	Usually no	More likely over time

Saving and investing solve different problems

Saving protects today. Investing protects tomorrow.

You need **both**, but you must use each correctly.

Investing — purpose, not jargon (Beginner meaning)

Investing means **putting money to work so it can grow over time** instead of staying idle. It allows your money to participate in economic growth — businesses expanding, jobs being created, and productivity improving.

For beginners, investing does not mean:

- Daily buying and selling
- Guessing the market
- Taking big risks

For beginners, investing simply means:

- Starting early
- Investing small amounts regularly
- Choosing simple, trusted options
- Staying invested for many years

In simple words: Saving keeps money safe. Investing helps money grow.

A simple map of common investment options (India)

India offers many investment options. You do **not** need to use all of them. This is only a **map**, not a checklist.

Investment option	What it means (very simple)	Mainly used for
EPF	Salary-based retirement savings	Salaried employees
PPF	Government-backed long-term saving	Safety-focused savers
Mutual Funds (SIPs)	Investing through professionals	Beginners & growth
NPS	Retirement-focused investing	Retirement planning
Stocks (long-term)	Owning parts of companies	Later-stage investors

Different tools solve different financial needs

Each option will be explained step by step in later chapters.

SIP — investing as a habit, not a shortcut

A **SIP (Systematic Investment Plan)** is a way of investing a fixed amount every month automatically.

It is popular with beginners because:

- You can start with small amounts (₹500 or ₹1,000)
- It removes the pressure of timing the market
- It builds discipline and consistency

Illustrative example (~12% assumed annual return):

Monthly SIP	20 years	25 years
₹500	~₹5 lakh	~₹10 lakh
₹1,000	~₹10 lakh	~₹20 lakh

Investing works best as a habit, not a shortcut

Returns are not guaranteed. The example only demonstrates *the power of time and discipline.*

The most important habit: pay yourself first

Rule:*Invest first, spend later.*

On salary day, move your investment amount before spending on lifestyle. Automation helps remove emotions and excuses.

Small, regular actions matter more than big, irregular decisions.

Common beginner thinking errors

Thought	Better approach
I earn too little	Start small; increase later
I will invest next year	Lost time never returns
Markets are risky	Lack of knowledge is the real risk
I'll save first, invest later	Do both together

Simple mindset shifts create better financial decisions

What you should do after this chapter

- Accept that saving alone is not enough for long-term goals.
- Decide a small monthly amount you can invest comfortably.
- Plan to automate this amount immediately after you receive your income.
- Keep emergency savings separate.
- Continue reading — clarity comes step by step.

End-of-Chapter Summary

- Inflation quietly reduces the value of savings.
- Saving and investing serve different roles.
- Investing is a long-term habit, not a gamble.
- Small monthly investing started early makes a big difference.

End-of-Chapter Checklist

- ✓ I understand why saving alone is risky long-term
- ✓ I know what investing means in simple terms
- ✓ I can name basic investment options
- ✓ I am ready to start small and stay consistent
- ✓ I will continue learning before acting

One-line lesson to remember

Save for safety. Invest for growth. Start small, and start now.

All examples are for learning purposes only and not personal financial advice.

CHAPTER TWO

Common Investment Mistakes Everyday People Make

Why Good People Make Bad Money Decisions

Most people who struggle with money are not careless, lazy, or irresponsible. They work hard, save regularly, and try to do what feels safe. Yet after 10–20 years, many still feel financially insecure.

The reason is simple: **small, repeated investment mistakes** quietly cancel out years of effort.

This chapter is not about blaming you.

It is about protecting you—from common traps that appear sensible on the surface but slowly weaken your financial future.

Most financial mistakes do not look like mistakes when they happen. They often feel reasonable in the moment. Over time, however, they quietly reduce your ability to build wealth.

Understanding these mistakes is the first step toward avoiding them.

A Familiar Moment: The Festival Buy

During a festival season, Raju's family celebrated with a new TV bought on an attractive zero-interest EMI. It felt like a smart and affordable decision.

Within months, an unexpected medical expense arrived.

Suddenly, the monthly cash flow became tight. The EMIs quietly reduced the money that had previously gone into small savings and investments.

The television brought temporary joy. The financial stress lasted much longer.

This is not a morality story. It is simply a common sequence:

Attractive offer → small EMI → reduced savings → lost investment opportunity

Over time, these small decisions shape long-term financial outcomes.

Another Familiar Story: The Honest Saver

Meena started working at 25. Every month, she saved in a savings account and fixed deposits because her parents always said:

"At least your money is safe."

By 40, she had built a respectable balance. But education costs, rent, and medical expenses had risen much faster than her savings.

She had been disciplined—yet still felt financially behind.

The mistake was not saving. The mistake was **stopping at saving.**

The Core Mistakes That Quietly Damage Wealth

Mistake 1: Starting Late Because the Amount Feels Too Small

Many people delay investing because they believe small amounts do not matter. They wait for a higher salary, a bonus, or the "right time."

Years pass while waiting.

In reality, **time is more powerful than the amount invested.**

Monthly Investment	Years Invested	Approximate Result*
₹1,000	25 years	~₹18–20 lakh
₹5,000	10 years	~₹10–12 lakh

Time matters more than starting big

Illustrative example assuming* ***moderate (~12%) long-term investment returns.*

The difference is not the monthly amount. The difference is the **years invested.**

The lesson is simple: ***starting early matters more than starting big.***

Better habit: *Start small, start early, and increase gradually as income grows.*

Mistake 2: Treating Saving as Investing

Savings accounts, FDs, and similar instruments protect money but rarely grow it meaningfully after inflation.

Tool	Purpose
Savings account	Safety & liquidity
FD / RD	Stability for short-term goals
Investments	Long-term wealth growth

Saving protects money. Investing builds wealth

Saving protects money. Investing grows money.

Both are important—but they serve different purposes.

Better habit: *Save for safety. Invest for growth.*

Mistake 3: Believing "Guaranteed" Products are Risk-Free

Many financial products feel safe because they promise fixed or guaranteed returns.

The hidden risk is **low growth over long periods**, which silently reduces purchasing power.

Money that grows slowly may appear safe today but can lose real value over time due to inflation.

Better habit: *Understand real risk. Losing purchasing power to inflation is also a risk.*

Mistake 4: Buying Lifestyle on EMI

Small EMIs for phones, gadgets, furniture, or comfort items often feel harmless.

But every EMI reduces future investment capacity.

A single EMI may seem manageable. Multiple EMIs slowly replace what could have been regular investments.

Better habit: *Never start an EMI that forces you to stop investing.*

Mistake 5: Emotional Reactions to Market Movement

When markets fall, fear encourages people to stop investing or withdraw money.

When markets rise quickly, excitement pushes people to invest aggressively at the wrong time.

These emotional reactions often lead to poor long-term outcomes.

Successful investing requires **discipline, not excitement**.

Better habit: *Investments work best when emotions are removed and discipline remains.*

Mistake 6: Chasing Tips and Quick Returns

Tips from friends, social media, news channels, or messaging groups often create temporary excitement.

They rarely create long-term wealth.

Many people enter investments late, after the initial gains have already happened.

Better habit:*Use simple, diversified options and stay consistent.*

Mistake 7: No Emergency Buffer

Without an emergency fund, investments are often **withdrawn** during financial crises.

This forces people to sell investments at the worst possible time.

An emergency fund acts as a financial shock absorber.

Better habit:*Build safety first, and then grow wealth steadily.*

Mistake 8: High-Cost Products and Complexity

Many complex financial products are difficult to understand and often carry higher costs.

Complexity frequently benefits the seller more than the investor.

In investing, simplicity often leads to better long-term results.

Better habit:*Prefer simplicity and transparency over complexity.*

Mistake 9: Mixing Trading with Investing

Short-term trading requires time, experience, emotional control, and a clear strategy.

Long-term investing requires patience and consistency.

Mixing the two approaches often creates confusion and poor decisions.

Better habit:*Keep investing boring and predictable.*

Mistake 10: Ignoring Small Money Leaks

Unused subscriptions, frequent impulse purchases, and convenience spending slowly drain money.

Individually these amounts appear small. Over years, they represent significant lost investment potential.

Small financial leaks can quietly delay long-term wealth creation.

Better habit:*Redirect small savings into consistent long-term investment habits.*

A Simple Protection Framework

Before any financial decision, ask:

- Does this reduce my ability to invest regularly?
- Does this create a long-term commitment for a short-term want?
- Am I deciding out of fear or excitement?

If yes—pause.

End-of-Chapter Summary

- Most mistakes are behavioural, not technical
- Small habits repeated over time matter most
- Safety and discipline protect long-term returns
- Simplicity beats complexity for beginners

End-of-Chapter Checklist

- ✓ I have started investing, even with a small amount
- ✓ I understand the difference between saving and investing
- ✓ I avoid lifestyle EMIs that stop investments
- ✓ I focus on consistency instead of excitement
- ✓ I review my habits instead of reacting to market movements

One line to remember

Wealth grows quietly when mistakes are avoided consistently.

All examples are illustrative. This chapter focuses on education, not personalised advice.

CHAPTER THREE

Investing vs. Trading vs. Gambling — Know the Difference Before You Start

One word, three very different meanings

Many beginners lose money not because markets are bad, but because they **confuse investing with trading**, or worse, unknowingly turn money decisions into gambling.

All three involve money and uncertainty, but their **purpose, mindset, and outcome** are very different.

Understanding this difference early will protect you from stress, loss, and disappointment.

A simple real-life situation

When Ajoy heard that his colleague had made quick profits in stocks, he opened a trading app. He bought shares without understanding the company or his goal. Prices fell, panic followed, and he sold at a loss.

Later, Ajoy started a monthly investment in a diversified fund and ignored daily market noise. Over the years, that simple habit quietly built financial stability.

Same market. Same person. **Different approach. Different results.**

What Is Investing? (Beginner meaning)

Investing means putting money into assets that can grow over time through patience and discipline, to meet long-term goals like education, retirement, or financial security.

Key characteristics:

- Long-term focus (5–30 years)
- Based on business or economic growth
- Uses time as an advantage
- Less frequent decisions

Example: Monthly investment into a diversified equity mutual fund for 15 years.

What Is Trading? (Beginner meaning)

Trading means buying and selling assets frequently to profit from short-term price movements.

Key characteristics:

- Short-term focus (minutes to months)
- Requires time, skill, and emotional control
- Higher stress and a higher chance of loss for beginners
- Results vary widely

Important note: Trading is not bad, but it is **not suitable for most beginners.**

What Is Gambling? (Beginner meaning)

Gambling means putting money at risk mainly based on luck, tips, or hope—without understanding or control.

Common signs:

- Decisions based on rumours, tips, or social media
- No clear plan or exit

- Emotional excitement or fear
- Repeated losses followed by "one last try"

Many people gamble unknowingly while believing they are investing.

Side-by-side comparison (simple table)

Aspect	Investing	Trading	Gambling
Time horizon	Long-term	Short-term	Very short-term
Decision base	Fundamentals & discipline	Price movement & skill	Luck & emotion
Stress level	Low	High	Very high
Suitable for beginners	Yes	Mostly no	No
Wealth building	High potential	Uncertain	Usually negative over time

Investing, trading, and gambling are not the same

A simple way to remember the difference

You can remember the three approaches using a simple idea:

- **Gambling → Luck**
- **Trading → Skill + Time**
- **Investing → Time + Discipline**

Most beginners underestimate how much skill and emotional control trading requires.

For everyday people with jobs, responsibilities, and limited time, investing usually provides the most practical path to building long-term wealth.

Why beginners should choose investing first

- Investing allows mistakes without destruction
- Time reduces risk
- Habits matter more than intelligence
- It fits normal jobs and family life

Trading demands attention. Gambling demands luck. **Investing demands patience.**

Common beginner traps to avoid

- Calling frequent buying and selling "investing"
- Using loan or emergency money for markets
- Checking prices daily and reacting emotionally
- Expecting fast results

These behaviours increase stress and reduce long-term success.

A protective rule for beginners

If you cannot explain why you are buying something in one calm sentence, you are probably not investing—you are speculating.

How to safely grow from here

For beginners:

1. Start with long-term investing habits
2. Learn basics slowly
3. Ignore short-term noise
4. Review progress once or twice a year

Trading, if ever attempted, should come **much later** and with separate money.

Looking Ahead

Understanding the difference is important.
But before you begin investing, one question matters —
can your financial life handle uncertainty without breaking?

Because knowing *what* investing is only solves half the problem.
If your finances are not stable, even the right investment can feel risky.

The real challenge is knowing **where to begin — simply, safely, and without confusion.**

In the next chapter, we'll explore the most practical starting points for beginners—so you can take your first step with clarity and confidence.

End-of-Chapter Summary

- Investing, trading, and gambling are not the same
- Confusion leads to loss
- Investing suits most everyday people
- Simplicity and patience protect capital

End-of-Chapter Checklist

- ✓ I know my goal before putting money anywhere
- ✓ I invest with a long-term view
- ✓ I avoid emotional decisions
- ✓ I do not confuse excitement with progress

One line to remember

Wealth grows from patience, not prediction.

All examples are illustrative and for educational purposes only.

Preparing Your Financial Foundation

Build safety and protection so investments are never forced, emotional or broken midway.

CHAPTER FOUR

Emergency Fund — Your First Investment

The fund that protects your peace of mind

Before money can grow, life must be stable.

An emergency fund may not look like an investment. It does not offer excitement, market stories, or visible growth. Yet, for most everyday people, it is the **most important financial decision they will ever make**.

An emergency fund protects something more valuable than returns — it protects your **calm, dignity, and ability to make good decisions** when life becomes uncertain.

A real-life moment: when plans meet reality

Suresh had done many things right. He saved regularly and had started investing with discipline. Then an unexpected job loss disrupted his income for several months.

Without an emergency fund, Suresh had only two choices:

1. break long-term investments at the wrong time, or
2. depend on loans and credit.

He chose survival over strategy. The loss was not just financial — it affected his confidence and peace of mind.

The mistake was not investing. The mistake was **investing without protection** first.

Situations like this are not rare. They are part of real life. That is why protection must come before growth.

What is an emergency fund? (Beginner meaning)

An emergency fund is money kept aside **only for situations you cannot plan for**, such as:

- Job loss or income interruption
- Medical emergencies
- Urgent family or home needs

It is not meant for vacations, gadgets, or lifestyle upgrades.

Simple meaning:*An emergency fund buys you time — and time protects your future decisions.*

Emergency Fund vs. Investment (Clear Difference)

Many beginners mix these two and pay a heavy price later.

Emergency Fund	Investment
Purpose is protection	Purpose is growth
Used during crisis	Used over long periods
Kept safe and accessible	Exposed to ups and downs
No focus on high returns	Returns matter over time

Protection and growth serve different purposes

Important:*Using investment money as emergency money often leads to forced selling and regret.*

Why an emergency fund comes before investing

An emergency fund:

- prevents panic decisions
- stops you from taking high-interest loans

- protects long-term investments from being broken
- gives confidence during uncertainty

In short, it protects both your **money and your behaviour**.

How much emergency fund is enough?

There is no perfect number. The goal is practical protection, not perfection.

Your situation	Recommended fund
Stable job, single income	3 months of expenses
Family depends on your income	6 months of expenses
Business / irregular income	6–9 months of expenses

Financial stability begins with preparation

Always calculate based on **monthly expenses**, not salary.
Protection is about covering what you spend, not what you earn.

Where should you keep your emergency fund?

The goal is safety and quick access — not maximum return.

Option	Why suitable
Savings account	Immediate access
Liquid mutual fund	Slightly better return, quick withdrawal
Short-term FD	Stability with limited lock-in

Emergency money should stay safe and accessible

Avoid placing emergency money in equity markets, long-term funds, or illiquid assets.

How to build an emergency fund (simple, realistic plan)

- Start with one month of expenses
- Set up automatic monthly transfers
- Increase slowly until target is reached
- Keep it separate from daily spending

Starting small is not a weakness. **Not starting is the real risk.**

Insurance is not a replacement

Insurance and emergency funds serve different roles:

- Insurance helps after an event
- Emergency funds help during the event

Both are necessary. One cannot replace the other.

After your emergency fund goal is achieved

This is a turning point where discipline matters most.

Once your emergency fund is complete:

- do not increase lifestyle expenses unnecessarily
- do not keep accumulating excess idle cash
- redirect surplus money into long-term investments (like SIPs)

This quiet shift is how stable people build wealth without stress. **Stability first. Growth second.** That order protects everything else in your financial life.

End-of-Chapter Summary

- An emergency fund protects peace of mind
- It comes before aggressive investing
- It prevents forced selling and bad loans
- Safety enables long-term growth

End-of-Chapter Checklist

- ✓ I know my monthly expenses clearly
- ✓ I am building my emergency fund consistently
- ✓ My emergency money is safe and accessible
- ✓ I will not use emergency funds for lifestyle wants

One line to remember

An emergency fund protects your future decisions before it protects your money.

All examples are illustrative and for educational purposes only.

CHAPTER FIVE

Insurance Before Investment — Life & Health

Protection first, then growth

Before you try to grow money, protect the people and plans that depend on it.

Insurance is not a way to make money. It is a quiet promise you make to your family — that if something serious happens, their life will not collapse financially.

Buying insurance is not exciting. There are no charts, no daily updates, no visible rewards. Just forms, policies, and small regular premiums. Yet this quiet decision is often the **single most powerful financial act of care** you will ever take.

Most people delay insurance not because they don't care, but because thinking about loss feels uncomfortable. This chapter exists to remove fear and confusion — and replace them with clarity.

This chapter explains insurance in plain language, clarifies why it must come **before aggressive investing**, and shares simple rules to help you decide how much cover you truly need. It also explains, calmly and honestly, why employer-provided cover is helpful but not enough.

A short, human story: the promise that was missing

Arun had started investing and felt proud of himself. SIPs were running. Savings were growing. Everything seemed on track.

Then a serious illness struck his partner.

Hospital visits turned into hospital bills. Daily expenses quietly increased. Arun stopped investments to manage cash flow. Savings began shrinking — money meant for the future now being used just to stay steady. Nights became sleepless — not only because of illness, but because every decision now carried pressure.

The illness would have been painful regardless. But without proper insurance, **financial stress became an extra burden the family did not need.**

If Arun had clear life and health protection in place, the situation would still be difficult — but calmer. Medical decisions could be made without panic. Long-term plans would not be sacrificed.

Insurance does not remove hardship.

It **protects dignity, choice, and stability during hardship.**

That is why protection must come before performance. That is its true role.

Insurance Is NOT an Investment (Read This Carefully)

This point is so important that it deserves special attention.

Insurance and investment serve **two completely different purposes:**

- **Insurance** exists to protect your family from financial shock.
- **Investment** exists to grow money over time.

When these two are mixed, both usually fail.

Many people buy insurance-linked products believing they are investing. The result is often:

- weak protection,
- slow growth,
- confusion during emergencies.

A healthy financial life keeps them separate:

- Buy insurance only for protection.
- Invest separately for wealth creation.

This simple separation prevents most beginner mistakes — and saves years of regret. "Many people learn this lesson only after a financial shock. Learning it early is an advantage."

What insurance really is (beginner meaning)

Insurance is a **risk-transfer tool.**

You pay a predictable, usually small, premium so that a large, unpredictable expense does not destroy your family's finances.

- **Life insurance** protects dependents if you die.
- **Health insurance** covers medical bills so savings remain intact.
- **Accident or disability cover** protects income if you cannot work.

Rule to remember:
Insurance protects your family's choices.
Investments create the wealth to use those choices.

Why insurance must come before serious investing

Without adequate insurance:

- You may be forced to sell investments at the wrong time.
- You may take high-interest loans during emergencies.
- Your family's standard of living can collapse after a single event.

With insurance:

- Investments continue working through difficult periods.
- Emergency funds and insurance together remove the need to borrow.
- You retain the power to choose — medical care, education, location — without financial panic.

This is not theory.
It is the difference between **calm response and financial crisis**.

Two simple essentials every household needs

For most beginners, focus only on these first:

- **Term Life Insurance** — pure protection for dependents.
- **Health Insurance** — covers hospital and treatment costs.

Everything else — endowments, ULIPs, add-ons — can wait.
Protection first. Complexity later.

Which Insurance Do I Need? (Quick Beginner Guide)

Situation	Need Term Insurance?	Need Health Insurance?
Single, no dependents	Optional	Yes
Married, spouse depends on income	Yes	Yes
Parents depend on you	Yes	Yes
Self-employed	Yes	Yes + higher cover

Protection needs change with responsibility

General beginner guide. Individual needs may vary.

Life insurance: what beginners must know

Who needs life insurance?

If anyone depends on your income — spouse, children, parents, or loan obligations — you need life insurance.

If no one depends on your income, life insurance can wait.

What Type to Buy First

Term insurance is the simplest, cheapest, and most effective option.

It pays a large amount to your family if you die during the policy term. There are no savings, no returns — only protection.

Why term insurance works best for beginners:

- High cover at low premium
- Transparent structure
- Easy to buy and understand

How Much Life Cover Do You Need? (Simple Rule)

A practical guideline:

Life cover ≈ 15–20 × your annual income, adjusted for loans and savings.

Monthly Income	Annual Income	Suggested Cover
₹25,000	₹3,00,000	₹45–60 lakh
₹40,000	₹4,80,000	₹75 lakh – ₹1 crore
₹60,000	₹7,20,000	₹1–1.5 crore

Adequate protection preserves family stability

To refine:

- Add future expenses (education, loans, living costs)
- Subtract liquid savings and employer cover

Example Cost (Illustrative)

A healthy 30-year-old buying ₹1 crore term cover may pay around **₹8,000–₹12,000 per year**, depending on insurer and health.

Buy early. Waiting increases cost — sometimes permanently.

Health insurance: why employer-provided cover is not enough

Employer health cover is helpful — but it often fails families when it is needed most:

- It usually stops if you change jobs.
- It may cover only the employee, not the family.
- The sum insured may be limited, with sub-limits and exclusions.

Pooja's story:

Pooja believed her company's ₹3 lakh health cover was enough. She was young, employed, and careful.

During a sudden hospitalisation, the total bill reached ₹6.5 lakh. At the payment counter, she realised her employer cover would pay less than half. The remaining amount came quietly from her savings — money meant for goals she had worked years for.

Nothing had gone "wrong." Yet the impact was immediate and deeply personal. The realisation stayed with her long after the hospital visit ended.

A few months later, Pooja bought a personal family health policy and a top-up. She did not buy it out of fear — she bought it for certainty. That decision ensured the next emergency would test health, not finances.

How Much Health Cover Is Enough?

Location	Minimum Base Cover
Small town	₹5 lakh
Tier-2 city	₹10 lakh
Metro	₹10–15 lakh

Health cover should match real medical costs

Tip: Buy a base family floater plus a top-up for higher coverage at lower cost.

What to Look for in a Health Policy

- No or low room rent sub-limits
- Strong cashless hospital network
- Pre- and post-hospitalisation coverage
- Clear waiting periods
- Transparent exclusions

Read the policy document before trusting it.

Do You Need Critical Illness or Disability Cover?

These covers provide lump sums during specific events.

Consider them if:

- You are the sole earner,
- You have limited savings,
- Your job involves physical risk.

Primary protection always comes first:
Life + Health > Everything else

Common insurance mistakes and how to avoid them

Mistake	Why it harms	What to do instead
Treating ULIPs / endowment as insurance	Low returns + high cost	Buy term insurance + invest separately
Relying only on employer health cover	Coverage disappears on job change	Buy personal family floater
Underinsuring because premiums are "expensive"	Big risk remains	Buy sensible cover now; increase as income grows
Letting policies lapse	Loss of cover + higher future cost	Set auto-pay; never lapse for small premium

Simple insurance decisions prevent future stress

The Right Order of Protection

1. Emergency fund
2. Term life insurance
3. Health insurance
4. Optional top-ups or riders
5. Long-term investments

Growth without protection creates stress. Protection before growth creates confidence. Protection builds the floor. Growth builds the future.

Practical First-Week Action Plan

- Calculate dependents and expenses
- Compare term insurance quotes
- Buy personal family health cover
- Set auto-pay
- Store policy details securely

When to Review Insurance

Review after:

- Marriage or child,
- Major loans,
- Income changes,
- Every 2–3 years routinely.

Increase cover gradually — not emotionally.

End-of-Chapter Summary

- Insurance is protection, not investment
- Term life + health cover form the safety net
- Employer cover is helpful, not sufficient
- Protect first, then grow

One Line to Remember

Insurance protects years of effort from one uncontrollable moment.

Simple Investment Options Explained Simply

Understand where to invest without fear, jargon, or dependency on experts.

CHAPTER SIX

Fixed Deposits, RD, PPF & EPF — Safe but Limited

Why safety feels comforting

For most people, their first relationship with money is built on safety.

We are taught early:

- Put money in a bank.
- Avoid risk.
- Don't lose what you have.

Fixed Deposits (FDs), Recurring Deposits (RDs), PPF, and EPF feel comfortable because they promise certainty. You know roughly how much you will get. You can sleep without worrying about daily market movement.

This chapter does **not** criticize these instruments. They play an important role in a healthy financial life. But they also have limits — and misunderstanding those limits can quietly slow your progress for decades.

The goal here is simple: to help you understand **where these instruments fit — and where they don't,** because confusion here can delay wealth creation for years.

Fixed Deposit (FD) — capital protection, not growth

A Fixed Deposit is a contract with a bank: you give money for a fixed period, and the bank returns it with interest.

Why people like FDs

- Capital feels safe
- Predictable returns
- Easy to understand

The hidden reality

FD returns often **barely beat inflation**, and sometimes don't beat it at all after tax.

Example (illustrative):

Item	Approximate Rate
FD interest	6–7%
Inflation (long-term)	~6%
Tax (for many earners)	reduces return further

Safety alone may not create real progress

Result: Your money is safe, but its **purchasing power barely grows.**

FDs protect money. They rarely build wealth.

Recurring Deposits (RD) — discipline without real growth

Recurring Deposits help people build a saving habit by depositing a fixed amount every month.

What RDs do well

- Build discipline
- Useful for short-term goals
- Simple and predictable

What RDs don't do

- They do not create meaningful long-term growth
- Returns are similar to FDs
- Inflation reduces real value over time

RDs are good **training tools**, not wealth creators.

PPF — safe, long-term, and patient

Public Provident Fund (PPF) is designed for long-term savers who value safety and tax benefits.

Why PPF is respected

- Government-backed
- Tax-efficient (EEE structure)
- Encourages long-term discipline

Limitations to understand

- Lock-in is long (15 years)
- Annual contribution limit exists
- Returns are steady but moderate

PPF works best as a **foundation layer**, not the entire building.

EPF — powerful, but not flexible

Employees' Provident Fund (EPF) is often the first real investment many salaried people make — sometimes without realizing it.

Strengths of EPF

- Forced monthly saving
- Employer contribution
- Tax advantages

Limitations

- Limited control
- Low liquidity
- Not sufficient alone for retirement

EPF is an excellent **supporting pillar**, not a complete retirement solution.

The silent risk most people ignore: inflation

Inflation slowly increases the cost of living over time.

Even when savings remain safe, their purchasing power may grow very little after inflation and taxes.

This is why fixed-return instruments provide stability — but may not be enough alone for long-term wealth creation.

This is why safety alone is not enough.

A simple comparison: purpose matters more than product

Instrument	Safety	Growth	Best used for
FD	High	Low	Short-term parking
RD	High	Low	Saving discipline
PPF	Very High	Moderate	Long-term stability
EPF	Very High	Moderate	Retirement base

Every safe instrument has a different role

Each tool has a role. Problems arise only when one tool is used for everything.

A Short Real-Life Story: The Patient Saver

Ramesh saved diligently in Fixed Deposits for nearly twenty years. He never missed a deposit. His balance grew steadily, and he felt secure knowing his money was safe.

When his child's higher education expenses arrived, Ramesh was surprised. The amount he had saved looked large on paper, but it covered far less than he had expected. Fees, accommodation, and related costs had grown faster than his savings.

Ramesh had done nothing wrong. He had been disciplined and patient. He simply relied on safety alone in a world where prices kept moving forward.

Safety protected his capital. It did not fully protect his future purchasing power.

When these instruments are useful

Use FD, RD, PPF, and EPF for:

- Emergency fund parking
- Short-term goals
- Stability portion of long-term plans
- Peace of mind

Do not expect them to:

- Beat inflation consistently
- Create significant wealth alone

Tax benefits & limits (simple view)

- **FD/RD**: Interest is taxable
- **PPF**: Tax-free returns, contribution limits apply
- **EPF**: Tax-efficient but rule-bound

Tax benefits help — but **tax-saving alone is not wealth creation.**

Where beginners go wrong

- Keeping all money only in safe instruments
- Ignoring inflation
- Delaying growth-oriented investments for too long

Safety should be the **starting point**, not the destination.

End-of-Chapter Summary

- Safe instruments protect money, not purchasing power
- FDs and RDs build discipline, not wealth
- PPF and EPF form a strong foundation
- Inflation is the real long-term risk

One line to remember

Safety keeps money alive. Growth helps it move forward.

CHAPTER SEVEN

Mutual Funds Made Easy for Beginners

Investing without fear

By now, you understand an important truth: **saving alone is not enough, and safety alone has limits.**

For many beginners, the term "*mutual fund*" creates unnecessary fear. It sounds technical. It feels risky. People imagine constant monitoring, complex decisions, or sudden losses.

In reality, mutual funds were created to solve a very simple problem:

How can ordinary people participate in long-term growth without becoming market experts?

This chapter is not meant to excite you or push you into investing. Its purpose is calmer and more important — to help you *understand* mutual funds, remove fear, and show how beginners can use them patiently and safely.

What is a mutual fund? (Beginner meaning)

A mutual fund is a pool of money collected from many investors.

This pooled money is managed by a professional fund manager, who invests it in shares, bonds, or a mix of assets according to the fund's stated objective.

Instead of buying individual shares yourself, you own **units** of the mutual fund. Your return depends on how the underlying investments perform over time.

Think of it simply:

- Many people contribute small amounts
- A professional manages the money
- Gains and losses are shared proportionately

Mutual funds **do not guarantee returns**. However, over long periods, they have historically helped patient investors grow money better than most fixed-return options.

Why mutual funds suit beginners

Mutual funds are designed for people who:

- Do not want to track markets daily
- Do not want to pick individual stocks
- Want diversification with small amounts
- Prefer professional management

One investment gives exposure to many companies or bonds. This reduces the risk of depending on a single investment or decision.

Mutual funds are not shortcuts — they are **structures built for consistency**.

Types of mutual funds (simple classification)

Beginners only need to understand three broad categories.

1. Equity Mutual Funds:

These funds invest mainly in shares of companies.

- Higher long-term growth potential
- Short-term ups and downs are normal
- Suitable for long-term goals (5+ years)

Equity funds are not gambling. They represent ownership in real businesses when held patiently. However, they can fluctuate significantly in the short term. Investors must be prepared for temporary declines. Ideally, equity mutual funds should be held for at least 5–7 years.

2. Debt Mutual Funds:

These funds invest in bonds, government securities, and similar instruments.

- Lower risk than equity
- More stable returns
- Useful for short- to medium-term goals

Debt funds help manage stability, not excitement.

3. Hybrid Mutual Funds:

Hybrid funds invest in both equity and debt.

- Moderate risk
- Balanced approach
- Suitable for cautious beginners

They provide a middle path for those easing into market exposure.

Direct vs. Regular plans — the simple truth

Every mutual fund offers two plans:

- **Regular Plan** — bought through a distributor or advisor
- **Direct Plan** — bought directly by the investor

The investment portfolio is the same. The difference is **cost**.

Regular plans include distributor commissions, which slightly reduce long-term returns. Direct plans have lower expenses and usually deliver marginally higher returns over time.

Beginner rule:

- If you are comfortable learning, choose **Direct**
- If you need guidance, **Regular** is acceptable — but understand the cost

SIP explained simply

A Systematic Investment Plan (SIP) allows you to invest a fixed amount at regular intervals, usually monthly.

SIP removes the pressure of timing the market and builds a habit of investing.

Example (illustrative):

- You invest ₹5,000 every month
- You buy more units when markets fall
- You buy fewer units when markets rise

Over time, the purchase cost averages out.

SIP is not about prediction. It is about **discipline and time.**

Example (illustrative):

₹5,000 invested monthly for 20 years at an assumed moderate annual return of around 12% could grow to approximately ₹50 lakh.

The total amount invested would be ₹12 lakh. The rest comes from compounding.

The growth comes from consistency and time — not prediction.

Why beginners should not fear market ups and downs

Market movements are normal.

What matters more than short-term movement is:

- Staying invested
- Continuing SIPs during downturns
- Allowing compounding to work

Most beginner losses happen not because of bad funds, but because of impatience. SIP sounds simple — and that is exactly why it works.

A Simple Example of Consistency at Work

Rakesh started investing ₹2,000 a month at 25 through a SIP.

He did not chase hot tips or try to time the market. Most years, he simply continued investing.

By 45, his investments had grown to around ₹25 lakh.

His income was ordinary. His plan was simple.

What made the difference was consistency.

He did not try to be clever. He simply stayed regular.

Over time, consistency quietly did what complexity often cannot — it built real wealth.

How beginners should choose mutual funds (simple guide)

Keep it simple:

- Choose funds with clear long-term objectives
- Prefer diversified equity funds or simple index funds
- Avoid chasing recent performance
- One or two funds are enough initially

Complex portfolios do not create better results for beginners. **Consistency does.**

Common mistakes beginners make

- Stopping SIPs during market falls
- Investing based on tips or trends
- Switching funds frequently
- Expecting quick profits

Mutual funds reward patience, not activity.

Where mutual funds fit in your financial life

Mutual funds are suitable for:

- Long-term wealth building
- Retirement planning
- Education and future goals

They are **not** substitutes for emergency funds or insurance. Growth works best when protection is already in place.

End-of-Chapter Summary

- Mutual funds pool money and invest professionally
- Equity, debt, and hybrid funds serve different purposes
- SIP builds discipline, not predictions
- Time matters more than timing

One line to remember

Mutual funds are not about beating the market. They are about staying invested long enough to grow with it.

CHAPTER EIGHT

Equity vs. Debt — Understanding Risk Without Fear

Why the word "risk" feels uncomfortable

By the time people reach this chapter, most already understand *what* to do with money — save regularly, insure properly, and invest patiently. What still holds many back is not lack of information, but fear.

The word **risk** does not feel like a number. It feels like danger. It feels like the possibility of losing hard-earned money, disappointing family expectations, or making a mistake that cannot be undone. Many of us grow up hearing well-meaning advice like *"Don't take risks"* or *"Markets are dangerous."*

But here is a quiet truth:

Most financial damage does not come from risk itself. It comes from misunderstanding risk.

This chapter is not about products or returns. It is about **how risk actually works**, why equity feels frightening, why debt feels comforting, and how time slowly transforms both.

Once this is clear, investing stops feeling like a gamble and starts feeling like a process.

What risk really means (simple meaning)

For beginners, risk is often confused with *loss*.

In reality:

- **Risk is uncertainty**, not permanent loss
- **Risk is movement**, not permanent destruction
- **Risk becomes dangerous mainly when time is ignored**

Temporary ups and downs are not failure. Panic reactions during those ups and downs usually are.

A useful way to remember this:

Volatility is emotional. Permanent loss is usually behavioural.

Debt — why it feels safe to the human mind

Debt-based options such as fixed deposits, bonds, and debt funds feel reassuring because:

- Returns are predictable
- Numbers do not change daily
- There is little emotional noise

Debt means you are **lending money** and earning interest. The experience feels calm and controlled.

Debt plays an important role:

- Protects capital
- Reduces anxiety
- Provides short-term stability

But there is a gentle truth worth understanding:

Debt feels safe because it rarely shocks you — but safety without growth quietly limits the future.

Debt protects capital. It does not always protect your long-term purchasing power.

Equity — why it feels scary (and why that fear is misleading)

Equity means **ownership** in businesses. When you invest in equity, you are not lending money. You are participating in growth — growth driven by people, innovation, productivity, and economic progress.

Why equity feels uncomfortable:

- Prices move every day
- Temporary losses feel personal
- Lack of control creates anxiety

What equity actually represents:

- Real companies
- Real products and services
- Growth that often keeps pace with inflation over time

A calm but powerful truth:

Equity is risky in the short term. Avoiding equity is risky in the long-term.

Equity does not require bravery. It requires **patience.**

Time — the most misunderstood factor in investing

Time quietly changes the nature of risk.

- Short time + equity = emotional stress
- Long time + equity = lower real risk

History shows that while equity markets are unpredictable in the short term, they have tended to reward patience over long periods.

Time does not remove ups and downs. Time removes the *danger* of those ups and downs.

Example (illustrative):

In a single year, equity markets can fall 20% or more.

Over 10–15 years, however, long-term trends have historically rewarded patient investors who stayed invested through volatility.

This is why equity is suitable for long-term goals, not short-term needs.

The invisible risk most people ignore: inflation

Many people fear market volatility but ignore a quieter risk — losing purchasing power over time.

Inflation does not create fear headlines or demand attention. Yet year after year, it changes what money can buy.

When returns only match inflation, effort is preserved — but progress is not.

This is why avoiding visible risk can expose you to **invisible risk**.

A simple mental model — stability and growth

Think of your financial life as having two layers:

- **Stability layer (Debt)** — protects today
- **Growth layer (Equity)** — protects tomorrow

Too much stability slows progress. Too much growth without protection creates stress.

Balance is not about excitement. It is about sustainability.

A Short Real-Life Story: Two Paths, Same Beginning

Anita and Sujit began their careers around the same time, earning similar incomes and saving with discipline.

Anita chose complete safety. She invested only in fixed-return options. Her money never frightened her, and for many years she felt peaceful and responsible.

Sujit felt the same fear but invested a small portion into equity for long-term goals. He did not check values often. Some years felt uncomfortable. Some years felt rewarding.

Years later, both had saved diligently. Anita's money was safe, but it struggled to keep up with rising costs. Suresh's money had grown faster, giving him more flexibility and options.

Neither was careless. Neither was reckless.

The difference was not intelligence. It was **time and exposure to growth**.

Common beginner misunderstandings about risk

- If markets fall, I lose everything
- Debt has no risk at all
- Equity is gambling
- I will invest after I feel confident

Confidence rarely comes first. Understanding and experience create confidence — not the other way around.

Where this understanding fits in your journey

So far, you have learned:

- How safety instruments work
- How mutual funds simplify investing
- How risk behaves emotionally and financially

The next step is learning **how to use equity in the simplest, least stressful way possible.**

That is where **index funds** come in.

End-of-Chapter Summary

- Risk is uncertainty, not loss
- Debt provides stability
- Equity provides growth
- Time reduces real risk
- Avoiding growth can be risky

One line to remember

Short-term fear is emotional. Long-term risk is structural.

CHAPTER NINE

Index Funds — The Simplest Smart Investment

Growth without complexity

By now, you understand two important truths.

First, safety alone cannot protect your future purchasing power. Second, equity is necessary for long-term growth — but fear and complexity often stop people from using it.

This is where index funds quietly solve a very real problem.

Index funds allow ordinary people to participate in long-term market growth **without stock picking, constant monitoring, or expert knowledge**. They are not exciting. They are not fashionable. And that is exactly why they work so well for beginners.

This chapter explains index funds in simple language — without hype, promises, or pressure.

What is an index? (Beginner meaning)

An index is a group of representative companies chosen to reflect a section of the economy or the overall market.

Instead of tracking one company, an index tracks **many companies together**.

Think of an index as a **report card of the economy**, not of any single business.

When the economy grows, the index tends to grow over time. When conditions are difficult, the index may fall temporarily.

Indexes rise and fall — but over long periods, they reflect the progress of businesses and productivity.

What is an index fund? (Simple explanation)

An index fund is a mutual fund that simply **follows an index.**

It does not try to predict markets. It does not try to beat other investors.

It follows one clear rule:

Invest in the same companies, in the same proportion, as the chosen index.

Your return closely matches the return of the index, minus a small cost.

The goal is not brilliance. The goal is **consistency**.

Why index funds are powerful for beginners

Index funds reduce three major risks that harm new investors:

- **Decision risk** — no stock selection or timing pressure
- **Cost risk** — lower expenses over long periods
- **Emotional risk** — fewer reasons to panic or overreact

They allow you to benefit from market growth while avoiding most beginner mistakes.

Index funds do not demand intelligence. They reward **discipline and patience.**

Index funds vs. Active funds (simple comparison)

Active funds try to outperform the market by selecting stocks. Index funds aim to **match the market.**

Aspect	Index Fund	Active Fund
Strategy	Rule-based	Manager decisions
Cost	Lower	Higher
Manager risk	Minimal	Present
Monitoring needed	Low	Higher

Simplicity often beats complexity over time

Some active funds perform well — but many fail to beat the market after costs, especially over long periods. Studies have shown that a majority struggle to consistently outperform broad market indexes after fees.

Index funds accept market returns — and avoid market mistakes.

Index mutual fund vs. ETF (Beginner clarity)

Index investing is available in two forms:

- **Index Mutual Funds** — invested via SIP or lump sum
- **ETFs (Exchange Traded Funds)** — bought and sold like shares

For beginners, index mutual funds are usually easier because:

- SIP setup is simple
- No need to watch market hours
- No trading decisions required

ETFs are useful only if you are comfortable operating a trading account and managing order execution.

How to start investing in index funds (Simple plan)

Keep the process boring and consistent:

- Choose one broad-market index fund
- Start a small monthly SIP
- Invest for long-term goals (minimum 5–10 years)
- Avoid frequent changes

Amount matters less than **consistency and time.**

How to choose an index fund (Practical checklist)

Look for:

- A well-known broad-market index
- Low expense ratio
- Low tracking error
- Stable fund house
- Simple SIP option

Avoid choosing based only on recent performance.

A Short Real-Life Story: Quiet Consistency

Neha started a small index fund SIP early in her career.

The amount felt insignificant. She did not track it closely or react to market news.

Years later, while reviewing her finances, she noticed something important. The money had grown quietly alongside her career—not instead of it.

There was no dramatic moment. Just confidence, stability, and relief.

The index fund did not make her rich overnight. It simply worked, year after year.

When index funds may not be suitable

Index funds are not ideal for:

- Short-term goals (less than 3 years)
- Emergency funds
- Investors seeking frequent trading excitement

Index funds reward **patience**, not activity.

Where index funds fit in your financial life

Index funds are suitable for:

- Long-term wealth building
- Retirement planning
- Education and future goals

They work best when combined with:

- Emergency funds
- Adequate insurance
- Disciplined investing habits

Growth works best on a **stable foundation.**

End-of-Chapter Summary

- Index funds follow the market, not predictions
- Low cost and simplicity reduce mistakes
- SIP builds long-term discipline
- Time matters more than cleverness

One line to remember

Owning the market calmly often works better than trying to outsmart it.

CHAPTER TEN

Stock Market Basics — Without Fear

Understanding without pressure

For many beginners, the stock market feels like a place meant for experts, fast traders, and people who enjoy constant risk. The first feeling is often fear — fear of loss, fear of making mistakes, fear of losing hard-earned money.

Understanding the stock market does not mean you must invest in individual stocks. Knowledge is safety, not pressure.

This chapter exists to make the stock market feel ordinary, understandable, and optional — not urgent. You will learn only what is necessary to remove fear, not to push action.

What is a share? (Beginner meaning)

A **share** represents a small piece of ownership in a company.

When you buy a share, you become a partial owner of that business.

- If the company grows and earns profits, the value of your share may increase.
- If the company struggles, the value may fall — sometimes only temporarily.

Think of it like owning a small slice of a bakery. If the bakery grows, your slice becomes more valuable. If business slows, the slice may be worth less for a while.

How shares are bought and sold — stock exchanges explained simply

Shares are bought and sold through organised marketplaces called **stock exchanges**.

In India, the two main exchanges are:

- **NSE (National Stock Exchange)**
- **BSE (Bombay Stock Exchange)**

You buy shares through a broker using a trading account. The shares are stored electronically in a **Demat account**.

This system is simply technical infrastructure. What matters more is how prices behave — and how investors emotionally react to them.

Why share prices move

Share prices move because of **demand and supply**.

Prices change due to:

- Company results
- Economic conditions
- News and expectations
- Investor emotions

A falling price does **not** automatically mean the company is failing. Very often it reflects short-term emotion, not long-term business value.

Shares vs. Mutual funds (Simple comparison)

Simple comparison:

Individual Shares	Mutual Funds
Require research	Professionally managed
Higher risk if undiversified	Diversification built-in
Emotionally stressful	Emotionally calmer

Mutual funds simplify stock market participation

For most beginners, **individual stocks are optional** — mutual funds are sufficient.

Common beginner mistakes

- Watching prices every day
- Acting on tips
- Expecting quick profits
- Investing without protection

Markets punish impatience more than lack of intelligence.

Simple safety rules

- Invest only long-term money
- Use SIPs for discipline
- Diversify
- Protect first (emergency fund + insurance)
- Review occasionally, not constantly

A Short Real-Life Story: Steady Learning

Rajib was curious about stocks but scared by news headlines. He started with a small SIP in an equity fund instead of buying individual shares.

Over time, his confidence grew. He realised he didn't need courage — he needed a **process**.

The investment continued quietly while his understanding improved.

Why beginners should start with mutual funds

Mutual funds:

- Reduce risk
- Reduce stress
- Reduce costly mistakes

They allow participation in growth without forcing expertise.

End-of-Chapter Summary

- A share is ownership in a company
- Markets move emotionally in the short term
- Mutual funds simplify stock market participation
- Protection and patience matter more than speed

One line to remember

The stock market rewards calm participation, not fearless action.

CHAPTER ELEVEN

Gold, Property & Other Assets — Understanding Alternatives Without Illusion

The attraction of "something solid"

When people feel uncertain about money or markets, they often look for something they can see, touch, or point to.

Gold can be held in your hand. Property can be visited and shown to others. Land feels permanent.

These assets create comfort not because they always perform better, but because they *feel real*. Visibility gives emotional reassurance — especially during uncertain times.

This chapter is not written to promote or reject gold or property. It exists to remove illusion.

Alternative assets **can support wealth** — but only when expectations are realistic and allocations sensible. When misunderstood, they often disappoint quietly over time.

What are "alternative assets"?

In simple terms, alternative assets are investments outside traditional bank deposits, bonds, and equity mutual funds.

Common alternatives many people consider:

- Gold (physical, digital, ETFs, SGBs, EGRs)

- Real estate (houses, flats, land)
- REITs (Real Estate Investment Trusts)
- Other assets (commodities, collectibles, niche investments)

These assets are often discussed emotionally — with stories of big gains or deep regret. The reality usually sits between those extremes.

Gold — protection, not prosperity

Gold has been valued for thousands of years. Its role has changed, but its purpose has not.

Gold is **not a growth engine.** It is a *stability tool.*

What gold does well

- Acts as a hedge during economic stress
- Holds value during extreme uncertainty
- Adds balance to a portfolio
- Carries cultural and emotional acceptance

Gold often performs best during periods of fear — not during strong growth phases.

What gold does not do well

- It does not generate income
- It does not compound like businesses
- Long-term returns often just match inflation

Gold preserves purchasing power. It rarely multiplies it.

Example (illustrative):

₹5 lakh invested in gold for 15 years may help preserve purchasing power during uncertain periods. The same ₹5 lakh invested in productive assets may grow meaningfully through long-term compounding.

How beginners should hold gold

Prefer financial forms over physical:

- Sovereign Gold Bonds (SGBs)
- Gold ETFs
- Gold Mutual Funds
- Electronic Gold Receipts (EGRs)
- Digital gold (with caution)

Heavy investment in jewellery usually leads to losses due to making charges and resale discounts.

Role of gold:*portfolio insurance, not the engine.*

Real estate — powerful, but demanding

Property is one of the most discussed and misunderstood investments.

Many believe property is always safe because prices "never fall." Reality is more complex.

Why property attracts investors

- Tangible and visible
- Potential rental income
- Long-term appreciation in good locations
- Emotional sense of ownership

The hidden demands of property

Property requires:

- Large upfront capital
- Long holding periods
- Maintenance and repair costs
- Legal and documentation awareness
- Patience during slow or flat markets

A good property decision can work very well. A poorly chosen one can lock capital for years with limited returns.

Property is **not passive.** It suits investors willing to stay involved.

REITs — real estate without ownership stress

REITs (Real Estate Investment Trusts) allow investors to participate in income-generating property without buying physical assets.

Why REITs suit beginners better than direct property

- Lower investment amount
- Regular income potential
- Higher liquidity than physical property
- Professional management

REITs behave more like income-focused investments than growth assets. They can **complement** a portfolio — not replace equity-based growth.

Other alternatives — proceed slowly

Assets like commodities, collectibles, or highly marketed new instruments often rise during hype cycles.

For beginners:

- Regulation may be unclear
- Pricing can be unpredictable
- Long-term history may be limited

A simple rule helps:

If you cannot clearly explain how an asset works, it may not be safe for your core money.

A Short Real-Life Story — Visible vs. Dependable

Meera felt proud owning a small plot of land on the city's outskirts. Family appreciated it. It felt like a smart and visible achievement.

Years passed. Development moved slowly. Paperwork, taxes, and uncertainty continued. The value did rise — but not meaningfully.

Meanwhile, her modest monthly investments in simple equity funds grew quietly. No visits. No calls. No documents.

The land was visible. The funds were quietly dependable.
Both had value — but only one worked silently in the background.

How much should alternatives form your portfolio?

For most beginners:

- Gold: **5–15%**
- Property / REITs: based on affordability and patience
- Core focus: equity + debt + safety instruments

Alternatives should **support**, not dominate, your financial life.

Common mistakes with alternative assets

- Over-allocating due to tradition or emotion
- Expecting gold to behave like equity
- Buying property without cash-flow planning
- Ignoring liquidity needs

Alternatives reward realism and patience. They punish emotional decisions.

Where alternatives fit in your financial life

Use alternatives for:

- Stability during uncertainty
- Diversification
- Emotional comfort (within limits)

Do not rely on them alone for:

- Retirement growth
- Long-term wealth compounding
- Emergency needs

End-of-Chapter Summary

- Gold protects value; it does not multiply it
- Property can work — but requires effort and patience
- REITs offer flexible property exposure
- Alternatives support portfolios; they don't replace fundamentals

One line to remember

Alternative assets bring balance — but growth still comes from productive assets.

CHAPTER TWELVE

Asset Allocation — The Art of Balance

Calm before the plan

Most people chase the "best" investment because uncertainty makes choosing feel urgent. That urgency usually comes from fear, not facts.

Here is a quieter truth that experienced investors learn slowly:

You do not need to be brilliant — you need to be balanced.

Asset allocation is the habit of dividing money by purpose so that no single event, market phase, or emotional reaction can damage your entire financial life. When allocation is right, decisions feel calmer, mistakes become rarer, and staying invested becomes easier.

This chapter is not about chasing returns. It is about building a structure that can survive uncertainty, emotions, and time.

What asset allocation really means (simple and practical)

Asset allocation is deciding **how much** of your money goes into different types of assets so that each portion has a clear job.

In simple words, it answers one question:

"How much money should go where — and why?"

Common asset groups:

- **Safety assets** — cash, FD, PPF, EPF (for stability and emergencies)
- **Growth assets** — equity mutual funds, index funds (for long-term wealth)
- **Stability / diversifiers** — debt funds, gold, REITs (to reduce shocks)

Asset allocation is structure, not activity. Once decided thoughtfully, it works quietly in the background.

Why balance matters more than finding the 'best' investment

Every asset has strengths — and blind spots.

- Safety assets protect capital but often lose to inflation
- Equity builds wealth but fluctuates emotionally
- Alternatives stabilise portfolios but rarely drive growth

Relying heavily on any single asset is not confidence. It is **concentration risk.**

Right allocation protects you from three common dangers:

- **Market volatility** — one fall should not pull everything down
- **Inflation** — too much safety quietly erodes purchasing power
- **Human behaviour** — fear and greed cause more losses than markets

Example (illustrative):

If equity falls 20% in a year but represents only half of your portfolio, the overall decline may be closer to 10%, not 20%. Diversification softens the impact.

Most long-term success does not come from clever moves. It comes from avoiding big, emotional mistakes.

A Quick Example — When Balance is Missing

Rahul invested most of his money in stocks during a market boom.

Everything seemed to be going up, and concentrating felt like the fastest way to grow wealth.

Then markets fell sharply — nearly 35%.

The decline was sudden and uncomfortable. Watching his portfolio drop every day created panic.

Unable to handle the pressure, Rahul sold his investments at a loss.

Priya approached investing differently.

She divided her portfolio:

- 60% equity
- 30% debt
- 10% gold

When markets declined, her portfolio also fell — but the impact was more manageable.

Because the fall did not feel overwhelming, she stayed invested.

Years later, her investments recovered and continued to grow steadily.

Lesson:

Balance does not just protect your money. It protects your behaviour when markets become uncertain.

The three-bucket framework — simple and memorable

Think of your money in **buckets, not bets.**

1. Safety Bucket — survival and peace of mind (0–3 years)

Purpose:

- Emergency needs
- Short-term expenses
- Mental comfort during uncertainty

Includes:

- Bank cash
- FD / RD
- PPF / EPF (partly, due to low liquidity)

This bucket ensures you never have to sell long-term investments in panic.

2. Stability Bucket — reducing shocks (3–7 years)

Purpose:

- Cushion during market stress
- Smooth portfolio ups and downs

Includes:

- Debt mutual funds
- Gold
- REITs

This bucket does not maximise returns. It protects behaviour.

3. Growth Bucket — building the future (5+ years)

Purpose:

- Long-term goals
- Retirement
- Beating inflation over time

Includes:

- Equity mutual funds
- Index funds

This bucket accepts volatility because time works in your favour.

The time ranges overlap intentionally. Life is flexible — your framework should be too.

A Short Real-Life Story — How Structure Creates Calm

Sujoy invested most of his savings in one asset that had performed well for years.

As long as returns were strong, everything felt easy.

But when that asset began to struggle, uncertainty followed.

Without a clear structure, every decision felt urgent.

Should he hold, sell, or switch? The lack of clarity created stress, and decisions became rushed and emotional.

Priya approached her money differently.

She divided her investments across safety, stability, and growth — each with a clear purpose.

Her portfolio did not grow the fastest in good years, but she rarely felt the need to react.

Nothing magical happened overnight.
What changed was not the market — it was the way decisions were made.
Structure did not remove uncertainty.
It removed confusion.

How to choose your allocation — the 3-question test

Before moving money, ask yourself:

- **When will I need this money?** (time horizon)
- **Can I emotionally tolerate a 20% fall without panic?** (risk tolerance)
- **Is this money meant for safety or for growth?** (purpose)

Longer time + emotional comfort → more growth exposure
Shorter time or discomfort → more safety and stability
If the answers feel unclear, lean towards balance — not extremes.

Example starting allocations (illustrative, not rules)

Profile	Safety	Stability	Growth
Conservative (near retirement)	50%	20%	30%
Balanced (mid-career)	30%	20%	50%
Aggressive (young, long horizon)	10%	15%	75%

Balance protects both money and behaviour

These are templates, not targets. Your life decides your mix — not tables.

Rebalancing — the quiet discipline that prevents panic

Markets automatically change your allocation. Rebalancing simply restores balance.

A simple rule:

- **Review once a year**
- If any bucket drifts significantly (around 10%), rebalance calmly

Rebalancing is not timing the market. It is discipline — trimming what ran ahead and supporting what fell behind.

Common asset allocation mistakes

- Chasing returns instead of structure
- Copying someone else's allocation blindly
- Ignoring emotional comfort
- Changing allocation too frequently
- Using allocation as an excuse to delay insurance or emergency funds

Asset allocation fails not because of math — but because of impatience.

Reflection question — one moment of clarity

Before changing anything, ask yourself:

Am I planning this allocation for purpose — or for comfort?

If comfort dominates, pause. If purpose leads, proceed.

A quiet lesson about balance

An experienced investor once shared a simple observation.

"In my early years, I spent a lot of time searching for the best investment. I believed success came from finding the perfect opportunity."

He paused and smiled.

"Years later, I realised something surprising. The investors who stayed calm the longest often did better than the ones who chased the most exciting ideas."

Markets change. Opportunities come and go.

But a balanced structure quietly does something more important — it makes staying invested easier.

Final Thought

The goal of asset allocation is not perfection.

It is stability — the ability to continue investing even when markets feel uncertain.

Looking ahead — from structure to goals

Asset allocation gives your money structure.
Goals give that structure direction.

Once your buckets are defined, each one can be linked to something meaningful — education, a home, retirement, or financial freedom.

This is where investing becomes personal.
It is no longer about percentages. It is about purpose.

A balanced portfolio helps you stay invested.
Clear goals give you a reason to stay committed.

In the next chapter, we will connect these two — turning your allocation into a plan built around the life you want to create.

End-of-Chapter Summary

- Asset allocation matters more than picking products
- Balance reduces emotional mistakes
- Safety, stability, and growth buckets simplify decisions
- Rebalancing maintains discipline

One line to remember

Asset allocation does not maximise returns — it minimises regret.

Goal-Based Investing (Most Important)

Link money to real-life goals instead of market noise or short-term returns.

CHAPTER THIRTEEN

Goal-Based Investing — Giving Your Money a Purpose

Money needs direction

Money without a goal creates confusion. Money with a goal creates calm.

Many people invest regularly yet still feel uncertain. They save, start SIPs, stop them, restart again, and constantly wonder: *Am I doing enough? Am I doing the right thing?*

The problem is rarely effort. It is the absence of clear goals.

Goal-based investing is not about chasing higher returns. It is about giving every rupee a **reason to exist**. When money has a purpose, decisions become easier, emotions become quieter, and discipline becomes natural.

This chapter shows how to connect your money to your life — simply, realistically, and without pressure.

What is goal-based investing? (beginner meaning)

Goal-based investing means investing **with a clear destination in mind.**

Instead of asking: "Which investment is best?"

You ask: "What is this money meant to do — and when?"

A goal answers three questions:

- **Why** am I investing this money?
- **When** will I need it?
- **How important** is this goal to my life?

Once these are clear, choosing investments becomes simpler and calmer.

A Short, Real-Life Picture — Busy but Unsure

Rohit invested in multiple SIPs because he was told it was the right thing to do. He checked balances often but could not explain what any fund was meant for.

When expenses increased, he stopped one SIP randomly. When markets fell, he paused another. Nothing dramatic went wrong — but nothing felt intentional either.

Rohit was investing. He was not **directing** his money.

Goals turn activity into intention.

Goals decide time. Time decides risk. Risk decides investment.

This simple chain explains most of investing.

- Goals decide **when** money is needed
- Time decides **how much volatility** you can accept
- Risk decides **which investments** are suitable

Example (illustrative):

If retirement is 25 years away, short-term market declines matter less than long-term growth. If a home purchase is just 2 years away, capital protection becomes more important than growth.

When people reverse this order — starting with products instead of purpose — confusion follows.

Three types of goals (human, not technical)

Instead of thinking only in financial terms, think in life terms.

1. Security goals — protecting stability

These goals protect your basic life structure.

Examples:

- Emergency fund
- Short-term stability needs
- Buffer for uncertainty

These goals need **safety and liquidity**, not high returns.
2. Life-building goals — growing forward
These goals help you build and improve life.
Examples:

- Children's education
- Buying a home
- Career or skill growth

These goals need **balanced growth** and patience.
3. Freedom goals — long-term independence
These goals shape your future choices.
Examples:

- Retirement
- Financial independence
- Legacy planning

These goals need **long-term growth assets** and emotional discipline.
Different goals can — and should — use different investment approaches.

How to define goals clearly (simple framework)

For each important goal, write down:

- **Purpose** — what the money is for
- **Time** — when it is needed
- **Amount (approximate)** — today's rough estimate
- **Monthly contribution** — what you can invest consistently

Precision is not required. Direction is enough.

Why goal-based investing reduces stress

When goals are clear:

- Market noise matters less
- Short-term falls feel manageable

- Decisions become goal-driven, not emotion-driven

You stop asking: "Is the market good or bad?"
And start asking: "Does this affect my goal right now?"
This shift alone prevents many costly mistakes.

Life in Motion: How Goals Grow Over Time

Goals are not separate from life — they grow with it.
The difference is not complexity, but consistency and time.

Consider Ratul's journey:

Starting Early

Age 25 → Starts ₹3,000 SIP
Age 30 → Increases investment after marriage
Age 35 → Begins planning for child's education
Age 45 → Portfolio crosses ₹1 crore
Age 60 → Retires with comfort and flexibility

Ratul did not rely on luck or a high income.
He simply started early, stayed consistent, and adjusted as life evolved.

Starting Late

Age 35 → Starts ₹5,000 SIP
Age 40 → Increases investment with income growth
Age 45 → Begins planning for child's education
Age 55 → Feels pressure as retirement approaches
Age 60 → Savings fall short of a comfortable retirement

Ratul did not make poor decisions.
He simply started late.

The Real Difference

Both paths required discipline.
Both involved effort.

But only one had time on its side.

When you start early, time does the heavy lifting.
When you start late, effort has to compensate — and often, it is not enough.

Goal-Based Investing Does NOT Mean

As Ratul's journey showed, investing is not about complexity — it is about staying aligned with your life.

Goal-based investing is powerful, but it is often misunderstood. Let's clear a few common misconceptions.

Not every goal needs a separate investment

You don't need:

- 10 different accounts
- 10 different funds

Instead, group similar goals and invest in a simple, organized way.

But one investment cannot serve every purpose

At the same time, not all goals can be combined.

Each goal has:

- A different timeline
- A different purpose

Using a single investment for everything can create confusion and risk.

The goal is not too many investments or just one — but the right structure for your goals.

Flexibility is still important

Life is unpredictable. Goals may change.

You can:

- Adjust timelines
- Increase or reduce investments
- Adapt to life events

This approach is a guide — not a rigid rulebook.

Constant goal changes create instability

Changing goals too often breaks consistency. Clarity and discipline matter more than frequent adjustments.

It's not about chasing the highest returns

Higher returns usually mean higher risk.

Your focus should be:

- Reaching your goal
- Not beating the market

Your plan should not be copied from others

Your goals are personal.

Blind imitation may look easy, but it often leads to regret.

Perfection is not required

You don't need:

- Exact numbers
- Perfect calculations

Start with rough estimates.

Clarity improves over time.

Market ups and downs are normal

Markets will fluctuate.

Stay focused on:

- Long-term goals
- Ignoring short-term noise

It doesn't have to be complicated

You don't need:

- Advanced strategies
- Constant monitoring

A simple, consistent approach is enough.
In simple words:
Goal-based investing is not about perfection or complexity.
It is about clarity, consistency, and staying aligned with your life.

How goals connect to asset allocation

Asset allocation is the **framework**. Goals give that framework **direction**.
The same person can have:

- Safe allocation for short-term goals
- Balanced allocation for medium-term goals
- Growth-heavy allocation for long-term goals

This is why goal-based investing feels organized — not restrictive.

A simple starting exercise (no calculations)

Take a piece of paper and write:

- One goal you must protect
- One goal you want to build
- One goal you want to grow into

Do not worry about amounts yet. Clarity comes before calculation.

Reflection before action

Before investing further, ask yourself:

Am I planning this money for comfort — or for purpose?

Comfort avoids thinking. Purpose creates direction.

A Quiet Truth

Goal-based investing is not really about money.
It is about giving your future a shape.

Without goals, money drifts —
it reacts, it pauses, and gets lost in noise.

With goals, money becomes quiet and purposeful.
It starts moving in a direction, even when life feels uncertain.

You may not always control markets.
You may not always get perfect returns.

But when your goals are clear,
you always know why you are investing —
and that clarity is what keeps you steady.

In the end, wealth is not built by chasing numbers.
It is built by staying connected to what truly matters in your life.

End-of-Chapter Summary

- Investing without goals creates confusion
- Goals decide time, risk, and investment choice
- Different goals need different approaches
- Goal-based investing reduces emotional mistakes

One line to remember

Money works best when it knows where it is going.

CHAPTER FOURTEEN

Investing for Children's Education — Planning with Time, Not Tension

Dreams need preparation, not pressure

Every parent dreams of giving their child the best possible education — not only good colleges, but freedom of choice.

Education is one of the most emotional financial goals. Fees rise faster than salaries. Decisions feel urgent. Many parents realise too late that goodwill alone cannot fight inflation.

Education planning is **not** about predicting what your child will become. It is about ensuring that when the time comes, money does not become the reason a dream is compromised.

This chapter shows how ordinary families can plan calmly — using time as an ally, avoiding panic later, and protecting both the child's future and the parents' financial stability.

A Quiet Moment Every Parent Recognises

One evening, Rajesh sat scrolling through a school brochure on his phone. The fees listed were higher than he expected — much higher. He did the math mentally, then closed the screen.

His child was still young. There was time. Yet a thought stayed with him: "*What if I don't plan early enough?*"

Nothing had gone wrong. No emergency. No crisis.

But that small moment revealed an important truth: **education choices are often limited not by talent, but by preparation.**

Why education needs early, time-based planning

Education costs grow faster than most household expenses. Even modest 8–10% annual increases in fees can double education costs in less than a decade. A course that costs ₹10 lakh today may cost significantly more in 10–12 years. The exact number is less important than the direction.

The biggest advantage parents have is **time.**

Time allows:

- Small monthly investments instead of large lump sums
- Compounding to work quietly
- Flexibility if plans change

Late planning removes all three — and replaces them with urgency.

Define the education goal clearly (simple framework)

Perfection is not required. **Clarity is.**

For each education goal, write down:

- **Purpose** — school upgrade, graduation, post-graduation, abroad studies
- **Time** — how many years away the expense is
- **Amount (approximate)** — today's rough estimate
- **Monthly contribution** — what you can invest consistently

Precision can come later. Direction must come first.

Time decides investment — the most important rule

Education planning becomes simpler when time is respected.

If the goal is more than 7 years away:

- Equity mutual funds or index funds
- Monthly SIPs
- Accept short-term ups and downs

Time absorbs volatility.

If the goal is 3–7 years away:

- Balanced or hybrid funds
- Reduced equity exposure

This phase is about protecting gains while still growing.

If the goal is less than 3 years away:

- Debt funds
- Fixed deposits
- Capital safety over returns

Never gamble with money needed soon.

A simple illustration (not a promise)

Suppose a parent invests:

- ₹5,000 per month
- For 15 years
- In a diversified equity fund

Total investment ≈ ₹9 lakh.

With time and discipline, the value can become significantly higher — not because of brilliance, but because of consistency and compounding.

Small amounts, started early, remove future stress.

Education loans — support tool, not a substitute for planning

Education loans are sometimes necessary — but often overused.

When loans can make sense:

- Part of the cost is already planned
- Course has strong long-term value
- Repayment will not strain family stability

When loans become traps:

- No prior saving exists
- Loan size decides the education choice
- EMIs create pressure during early career years

Planning reduces dependence. Loans should support ambition — not create fear.

A Short Real-Life Contrast — Early vs. Late

Mampi started a small SIP when her daughter was five. The amount felt insignificant. She increased it gradually as income grew.

Ravi planned to save later, once his salary improved. Years passed faster than expected.

When college admissions arrived, Meena had options. Ravi had urgency.

Neither lacked love or intent. Only one respected time.

A child's dreams should not be delayed because planning was delayed.

What you save quietly today may become their freedom tomorrow.

Should education investments be in the child's name?

For simplicity and flexibility:

- Investments can remain in the parent's name
- Goal tagging matters more than account ownership

Control, tax efficiency, and discipline usually remain better with parents.

Common mistakes parents make

- Starting late
- Investing too conservatively for long horizons
- Stopping SIPs during market falls
- Mixing education money with other goals
- Breaking retirement savings for education

Education is a priority — but not at the cost of long-term family stability.

How education planning fits into your overall plan

Education planning works best when:

- Emergency fund is in place
- Insurance is adequate
- Asset allocation is balanced

Education goals should **not compete** with retirement goals. Both deserve protection.

End-of-Chapter Summary

- Education costs rise faster than inflation
- Time is the biggest advantage parents have
- Equity suits long-term education goals
- Loans should support, not replace planning
- Small, early SIPs reduce future pressure

One line to remember

Start early, invest calmly — and let time educate your money before your child needs it.

CHAPTER FIFTEEN

Marriage & Big Life Expenses — Celebrating Life Without Breaking the Future

Joy should not become long-term pressure

Marriage, celebrations, relocations, and major family milestones are meant to be remembered with happiness — not with financial stress that quietly follows for years.

Across cultures, these events carry emotional and social expectations. In the moment, spending feels justified — once-in-a-lifetime, unavoidable.

Many people realise only later a simple truth:

The real cost of big life expenses is not the money spent — it is the years of financial progress quietly erased.

This chapter is not about reducing joy or celebration. It is about protecting your future while honouring important moments today — calmly, respectfully, and without regret.

Why big life expenses derail even disciplined investors

Big life expenses differ from daily spending in three important ways:

- They feel urgent and unavoidable
- They are emotionally charged
- They are socially visible

Because of this, good investors often make avoidable decisions:

- Breaking long-term investments
- Using emergency funds for non-emergencies
- Borrowing at high cost without a clear plan

The damage rarely shows immediately. It appears later — as delayed goals, lost compounding, and prolonged financial recovery.

Celebrations last days. Financial impact can last years.

A Familiar Picture — The Celebration Hangover

Anil had been investing regularly for six years. When marriage planning began, expenses increased gradually — clothing, functions, travel, gifts. None felt excessive on its own.

To manage cash flow, he paused SIPs. Later, he withdrew long-term investments. After the wedding, restarting felt difficult — priorities had shifted and expenses had permanently increased.

The marriage brought happiness. The financial after-effects lasted much longer.

Planning earlier would not have reduced joy — it would have reduced stress.

The invisible cost nobody talks about

When money is spent on big events, the visible cost is the bill.

The invisible costs are:

- Compounding that never happened
- SIPs that were stopped and never restarted
- Retirement years pushed further away
- Emotional stress long after the celebration ends

These costs do not appear on invoices — but they shape your financial future.

The golden rule of big expenses

Never fund permanent goals with temporary emotion.

Marriage and celebrations are temporary moments.

Your retirement, children's future, and financial independence are permanent responsibilities.

Short-term happiness should not permanently weaken long-term security.

Loans for celebration — where caution is essential

Loans for weddings and big events are often marketed as harmless:

- Small EMIs
- Celebrate now, pay later
- Easy approvals

EMIs hide the true cost:

- Long repayment periods
- Interest draining future cash flow
- Reduced ability to invest consistently

Loans may support essential needs. For celebrations, however, they require extreme caution.

If borrowing is unavoidable, ensure it is:

- Limited
- Short-term
- Fully planned for repayment

Debt should support planning — never replace it.

A healthier approach — plan, don't perform

Healthy planning does not mean minimal celebration. It means intentional celebration.

Better approaches include:

- Fixing a spending range early
- Creating a separate celebration fund
- Protecting emergency and retirement savings
- Choosing memories over displays

Planning does not remove joy — it protects it.

How to plan big expenses without harming investments

Use a simple three-layer approach:

1. Separate the celebration fund

Create a dedicated savings bucket using:

- Recurring deposits
- Short-term debt funds
- High-liquidity savings

This prevents accidental withdrawals from long-term investments.

2. Respect the time horizon

- 3–5 years away → Small monthly savings
- 1–3 years away → Capital protection focus
- Less than 1 year → No market exposure

Markets are not emergency tools.

3. Decide the limit before emotion enters

Fix how much is enough before discussions begin. A predefined limit reduces:

- Social pressure
- Comparison-driven spending
- Post-event regret

Big expenses and social expectations

Spending decisions often feel personal — but they are rarely private.

A balanced mindset:

- Respect traditions
- Respect relationships
- Respect your future equally

Quiet financial discipline today protects dignity tomorrow. You do not need to explain every boundary.

How this chapter connects to retirement

Many people damage retirement not through bad investments — but through unplanned life expenses.

What feels like a one-time decision often silently reduces:

- Long-term compounding
- Future independence
- Choice in later life

Protecting retirement starts long before retirement planning begins.

End-of-Chapter Summary

- Big life expenses need planning, not pressure
- The biggest cost is lost future progress
- Separate celebration funds protect investments
- Loans for celebration require extreme caution
- Financial discipline protects both joy and stability

One line to remember

Celebrate your milestones — but never at the cost of your future freedom.

CHAPTER SIXTEEN

Retirement Planning for Common People — Freedom Is Built Quietly

Retirement is Not Optional

Retirement is not a luxury reserved for the wealthy. It is a responsibility every earning person carries — whether they acknowledge it or not.

The fear around retirement is rarely about money alone. It is about losing independence — about becoming dependent when independence once defined your life.

Many people delay retirement planning because it feels distant, complicated, or intimidating. Others assume they will "manage somehow" when the time comes.

In reality, retirement does not arrive suddenly. It is built — quietly — through small, repeated decisions made during working years.

This chapter is not about numbers or predictions. It is about responsibility, dignity, and choice.

What retirement planning really means (simple meaning)

Retirement planning is not about stopping work. It is about having the choice not to be forced to work.

It means having the ability to choose:

- Whether to continue working or not

- How to live, not just where to survive
- How much to depend on others — or not at all

At its core, retirement planning answers one question:

"How will I support my life when my regular income stops?"

That support does not come from one decision. It comes from consistency.

Why retirement is everyone's responsibility

In earlier generations, joint families, pensions, or fixed employment often provided support. Today, most people must build their own safety.

Common assumptions that quietly fail:

- Children will take care of us
- Property will be enough
- Something will work out

Sometimes these hopes come true. Often, they create pressure — on family, on relationships, and on self-respect.

Planning for retirement is not pessimism. It is consideration — for yourself and for those you love.

The real cost of not planning (without fear)

The cost of ignoring retirement planning is not always poverty.

More often, it is lost choice.

Lost choice about:

- Where you live
- How you spend your time
- Whether medical or financial decisions feel stressful

Money gives options. Lack of planning removes them quietly.

Retirement is built by small habits, not big decisions

Many people believe retirement requires large investments. In reality, it is built by small monthly discipline.

What matters most:

- Starting early
- Staying consistent
- Avoiding long breaks
- Letting time do the heavy work

Retirement wealth is rarely built by dramatic decisions. It is built by small decisions that were never stopped.

Time is the most powerful factor

Time reduces pressure.

Someone who starts early can:

- Invest smaller amounts
- Take sensible growth exposure
- Recover from market fluctuations
- Adjust plans gradually

Someone who starts late:

- Feels urgency
- Takes emotional risks
- Depends heavily on predictions
- Has little room for correction

Retirement planning rewards patience, not intelligence.

A simple example shows how powerful time can be:

A few years of delay can dramatically increase the monthly amount required. Consider this example:

To Build ₹1 Crore by Age 60

Start Age	Approx Monthly SIP Needed
25	₹1,500
35	₹5,000
45	₹20,000

Time is the biggest advantage in investing

Illustrative example only. Actual returns and needs may vary.

Time can reduce the burden — but once lost, it becomes expensive to replace.

Two Neighbours, Two Different Retirements

Mr. Sharma worked hard for more than 35 years.

He was responsible, avoided unnecessary risks, and believed that saving money in fixed deposits was the safest option. Every year, he added some savings to his bank deposits. When he finally retired, he had a reasonable amount of money set aside.

But life after retirement was not as comfortable as he had imagined. Prices had risen steadily over the years. Medical expenses were higher than expected. His savings grew slowly, and inflation quietly reduced the real value of his money.

Mr. Sharma often found himself worrying about whether his savings would last.

In the same neighbourhood lived his friend, Mr. Shetty.

Mr. Shetty did not earn a much higher salary than Mr. Sharma. But many years earlier, he had started small monthly investments through SIPs in mutual funds.

The amounts were modest at first. Sometimes just a few thousand rupees a month. But he stayed consistent for decades. Over time, the power of compounding worked quietly in the background.

By the time Mr. Shetty retired, his investments had grown far beyond what he had originally imagined. His retirement income felt stable, and he had the freedom to enjoy his time without constantly worrying about money.

Both men worked hard for their families.

The difference was not income. The difference was **time and the way their money was allowed to grow.**

This is why retirement planning is not about earning a very high salary. It is about starting early, investing patiently, and giving your money enough time to grow.

Where retirement fits in your financial structure

Retirement planning works best when:

- Emergency fund is already in place
- Insurance protects against major shocks
- Other goals are planned separately

Retirement should not compete with:

- Children's education
- Major celebrations
- Short-term lifestyle upgrades

It deserves its own protected space.

Common mistakes people make with retirement

- Treating retirement as optional
- Starting only after major life expenses
- Stopping investments during temporary stress
- Using retirement funds for non-emergencies

- Expecting one asset to do everything

Retirement planning fails not due to markets — but due to interruptions.

How much is "enough"? (the honest answer)

This is the most common — and most misunderstood — retirement question.

The honest answer is simple:

There is no single "enough" number that applies to everyone.

Enough depends on:

- Lifestyle expectations
- Healthcare needs
- Family responsibilities
- Location and cost of living
- Inflation and time

Instead of chasing a final number, focus on:

- **Consistency** — investing every month
- **Coverage** — emergency fund and health insurance
- **Progress** — increasing contributions when income grows
- **Review** — adjusting plans every few years

Retirement planning is not about hitting a perfect number. It is about **reducing future dependency and increasing future choice.**

If your future self has:

- Regular income flow
- Medical expenses covered
- Basic lifestyle protected
- Freedom to say "no" when needed

You are closer to "enough" than you think.

A calm reflection

Ask yourself — honestly, without fear:

"Am I planning retirement to look rich — or to live peacefully?"

Peace requires less perfection than people imagine.

A Quiet Reminder Before You Move Ahead

A retired teacher once said something simple but powerful.

"When I was young, retirement felt very far away. I always believed there would be enough time later to start planning."

He paused for a moment and then added,

"Years passed faster than I expected. The only thing I regret is not starting earlier."

Money decisions rarely feel urgent when we are young.

But retirement arrives whether we prepare for it or not.

Final Thought

The goal of retirement planning is not luxury.

It is peace of mind — the freedom to live your later years without financial stress.

And that freedom is built slowly, through small decisions made many years earlier.

The Next Step — Protecting Your Retriement

Understanding the importance of retirement is only the first step.

The real question is — where should you invest to make this future possible?

In the next chapter, we will explore that.

End-of-Chapter Summary

- Retirement planning is a responsibility, not a luxury
- The true goal is independence and choice
- Small, consistent habits matter more than large actions
- Time is the greatest advantage
- Retirement freedom is built quietly, long before retirement arrives

One line to remember

Retirement freedom is not created at 60 — it is protected quietly at 30, 35, and 40.

Practical Action Plan

Convert knowledge into a simple, repeatable investing system.

CHAPTER SEVENTEEN

How to Start Investing — Step by Step (Without Confusion)

Starting matters more than perfection

Most people do not fail at investing because of wrong choices.
They fail because they never start — or because starting feels confusing and intimidating.

This chapter is written to remove that confusion.

You do not need advanced knowledge. You do not need a large amount of money. You do not need everything on Day One.

You only need clarity about what is mandatory, what is optional, and what can wait.

Once the basic setup is done, investing becomes simple — even boring. And that is exactly how it should be.

Step 1: PAN Card — your financial identity

A PAN (Permanent Account Number) is the foundation of investing in India.
It links your investments, income, and taxes under one identity.

PAN is mandatory for:

- Mutual funds
- Shares, ETFs

- NPS
- Most taxable investments

Without PAN, market-linked investing is not possible.
Important clarity (very common doubts):

- PAN is mandatory for **PPF**
- PAN is not always mandatory for small bank FDs, but linking PAN is strongly recommended

If you do not have a PAN card, this is your first step. Everything else comes later.

Step 2: Bank account — the money highway

Your bank account is where:

- Money comes from (salary / business)
- Investments go out
- Returns come back

For investing, ensure:

- Account is active and in your own name
- Mobile number is linked
- Net banking is enabled

A normal savings account is enough.
You do not need a special "investment account" to begin.

Step 3: KYC — one-time compliance

KYC (Know Your Customer) is a legal requirement to prevent fraud.
It usually requires:

- PAN
- Address proof
- Identity verification

Once completed, KYC generally works across:

- Mutual funds
- Brokers
- Most investment platforms

This is a **one-time process**, not something you repeat every year.

Demat account vs. Mutual Fund account — the confusion most beginners have

This misunderstanding stops many people from starting.

Demat Account

- Holds shares, ETFs, bonds in electronic form
- Required for direct stock market investing
- **NOT mandatory for mutual fund SIPs**

Mutual Fund Account

- Holds mutual fund units
- Can be opened **without** a Demat account
- Fully sufficient for SIPs and long-term investing

Clear answer to a common question:

- No, a Demat account is **NOT required** to start SIPs in mutual funds.

Demat is optional unless you want to buy shares or ETFs directly.

Fixed-income investments — Demat & PAN clarity

For instruments like:

- PPF
- EPF
- NPS
- Bank FDs

- Post Office schemes

Key points:

- Demat account is **NOT required**
- PAN is mandatory for **PPF and NPS**
- PAN is recommended (and often required) for higher-value FDs

These instruments focus on safety and structure rather than market participation.

What you actually need to start (simple checklist)

Mandatory

- PAN card
- Bank account
- Completed KYC

Optional (based on goals)

- Mutual fund account — for SIPs and long-term investing
- Demat account — only if you want stocks or ETFs

You do **not** need:

- Multiple apps
- Multiple accounts
- Expert predictions
- Large capital

Simple setups last longer.

Common beginner mistakes to avoid

- Opening many apps at once
- Buying products before defining goals
- Assuming Demat is compulsory for everything
- Starting investments before building an emergency fund
- Copying others without understanding purpose

Clarity beats speed.

A calm reminder before you move ahead

You are not late.
You are not behind.
You are not unprepared.
Once this basic structure is ready:

- Fear reduces
- Decisions become easier
- Discipline becomes natural

Investing success starts with clarity, not complexity.

End-of-Chapter Summary

- PAN, bank account, and KYC form the foundation
- Demat account is optional for mutual fund SIPs
- Fixed-income investments do not need Demat
- You do not need everything at once
- Correct setup matters more than fast action

One line to remember

You don't need to start big — you need to start correctly.

CHAPTER EIGHTEEN

The Three-Bank-Account System — Smart Control Without Stress

Why money feels out of control

Many people earn regularly, save occasionally, and invest with good intentions — yet still feel that money slips away.

The problem is rarely income — and rarely a lack of discipline. The real problem is mixing purposes.

When salary, spending, UPI payments, credit cards, SIPs, EMIs, insurance premiums, and savings all flow through one bank account, clarity disappears. You never know:

- How much is safe to spend
- How much is already committed
- How much belongs to the future

This chapter introduces a simple system used quietly by financially calm people: the **Three-Bank-Account System**.

It does not increase income. It does not restrict life. It simply creates structure — and **structure creates peace.**

Why one bank account creates silent chaos

Using one account for everything creates invisible stress:

- SIPs compete with lifestyle spending
- Credit card bills arrive unexpectedly
- Emergency funds get used casually
- Investments stop during short-term pressure

Nothing dramatic happens in one month. The damage appears slowly — through inconsistency.

Money needs boundaries to behave well.

The core idea — money needs roles, not willpower

Instead of controlling every expense emotionally, this system assigns **roles** to money.

Each account has one clear job. No account tries to do everything.

When money has clear roles, discipline becomes automatic — not forced.

Account 1: Salary / Income Account — the distribution hub

This is where your income first arrives.

Purpose:

- Receive salary or business income
- Distribute money to other accounts

Rules:

- Do not use this account for spending
- No UPI linked
- No debit or credit card payments

Within a few days of receiving income, money should move out to:

- Expense Account (for living)
- Investment Account (for the future)

This account is a junction — not a destination.

Account 2: Expense Account — your life account

This account supports daily living.

Purpose:

- Monthly expenses
- Lifestyle spending
- Bills, groceries, rent, fuel, subscriptions

Golden rule:

UPI, debit cards, and credit card payments must be linked ONLY to this account.

This creates a natural spending boundary.

When this account's balance falls, spending slows automatically — without guilt or panic.

This is controlled freedom.

Credit cards — tool, not trap

Credit cards are not income. They are delayed cash.

Correct usage:

- Swipe only for expenses
- Pay the full bill every month
- Pay from the Expense Account

Never:

- Pay credit card bills from investment accounts
- Convert lifestyle spending into long EMIs

Golden rule:

If you cannot pay the credit card bill from your expense account, the expense was too big.

UPI — powerful convenience with boundaries

UPI makes spending frictionless — which is why it needs structure.

Linking UPI only to the Expense Account:

- protects investments automatically
- prevents impulse use of savings
- keeps spending visible and contained

UPI is not dangerous. **Unlimited access is.**

Insurance linkage — often ignored, very important

Insurance premiums should not disturb daily cash flow or long-term investments.

A simple approach:

- Term insurance premiums → Expense Account (planned yearly expense)
- Health insurance premiums → Expense Account

The key is **predictability**. Insurance should feel routine — not like a sudden financial shock.

Never fund insurance premiums by breaking investments.

Account 3: Investment Account — your future account

This account exists for one purpose only: **building your future.**

Purpose:

- SIPs
- RDs
- Long-term investing

Rules:

- No debit card
- No UPI
- Auto-debit enabled

Money in this account should feel non-spendable.
This psychological separation is more powerful than budgeting apps.

Where the emergency fund fits

Emergency money should be:

- Liquid
- Visible
- Easy to access

Options:

- Separate savings account
- Sub-account linked to expense account

Never mix emergency funds with:

- Investment accounts
- Credit card usage
- Lifestyle spending

Top-up rule (simple):
If the Emergency balance drops below your target, refill it from the Income Account on the next payday — before increasing lifestyle spending.

Emergency money protects dignity. It prevents temporary problems from becoming long-term damage.

A Short Real-Life Contrast — Same Income, Different Calm

Two people earn the same salary.

One uses a single account. Money feels tight. SIPs stop frequently. Credit card bills arrive as surprises.

The other uses three accounts. Spending feels lighter. SIPs run quietly. Emergencies stay contained.

The difference is not income. **It is structure.**

One-weekend setup plan

- Open or repurpose three accounts
- Ensure salary is credited to the Income Account.
- Automate transfers to the Investment Account and Emergency Buffer on or immediately after payday.
- Move SIP auto-debits to the Investment Account.
- Link cards and UPI only to the Expense Account.
- Review after one month and adjust percentages.

Freelancer / Irregular Income Tip:

If income varies, build a larger buffer (4–9 months of expenses). Whenever you receive income, transfer a fixed percentage — not a fixed amount — to your Investment and Emergency accounts. Always fund the current month's expenses first.

Three-Account Flow — Salary → Split → Spend & Secure

Split your pay within 2–3 days so spending, saving and safety do not mix.

Salary / Income Account

↓

Split (within 2–3 days)

↓ ↓

Expense Account | Investment Account

↓

Emergency Buffer (visible & liquid)

Every rupee should have a purpose

How it works:

Salary arrives → split it within 2–3 days → Expense handles daily life → Investment runs SIP auto-debits → Emergency remains liquid and untouched unless truly needed.

This distribution repeats every month — automatically.

Example (illustrative):

If monthly net salary is **₹50,000 → ₹30,000 Expense | ₹10,000 Investment | ₹10,000 Emergency.**

Adjust proportions based on EMIs, dependents, or income variability.

End-of-Chapter Summary

- One account creates confusion
- Three accounts create automatic discipline
- UPI and credit cards belong only to the Expense Account
- Investment money must remain protected
- Structure reduces stress without reducing joy

One line to remember

Money behaves better when it knows where it belongs.

CHAPTER NINETEEN

Credit Cards — Use as a Tool, Not a Trap

Power without discipline becomes danger

Credit cards are neither good nor bad. They are powerful.

And power without discipline quietly turns into damage.

For some people, credit cards improve cash flow, build credit history, and add convenience. For many others, the same card becomes a source of stress, revolving debt, and silent financial leakage.

The difference is not income. It is mindset and structure.

This chapter teaches how to use credit cards as a **tool** — not a lifestyle upgrade, not an emergency fund, and never as hidden income.

What a credit card really is (simple truth)

A credit card is borrowed money with a short grace period.

It is not:

- Extra income
- A reward for spending
- A solution to cash shortage

It is a **30–50 day, interest-free loan** — nothing more. Every swipe is a temporary loan that must be repaid **fully and on time** — or it becomes very expensive.

The clearer you are about this, the fewer mistakes you will make.

The single mindset that changes everything — the debit-card mindset

Treat your credit card **as if it were a debit card.**

That means:

- Spend only what already exists in your bank account.
- Use the card for timing convenience, not to afford things you cannot pay for now.
- Assume the bill is already spent money the moment you swipe.

Mentally deduct it from your bank balance immediately — even before the statement arrives.

Interest on credit cards is among the highest in personal finance. If you cannot pay the full bill comfortably from your Expense Account, the purchase was too large.

Why minimum payments and cash withdrawals are traps

Minimum due is not safety — it is slow debt. Paying only the minimum turns small spends into long-term burdens. What feels manageable today becomes expensive tomorrow.

Cash withdrawal on a credit card is a different trap: it attracts immediate interest and high fees with no grace period. It converts a simple need into expensive debt instantly.

Golden rule:

If you cannot pay the full bill this month, do not swipe.

Linking cards to your money system — the hard boundary

From Chapter 18: credit cards must be linked **only** to the Expense Account. Never to salary, savings, or investment accounts.

Why this boundary matters:

- Expenses stay visible and contained.
- Credit-card bills come from the account that pays for daily life — not from future wealth.
- Auto-debit rules and controls are easier to enforce.

This one rule protects SIPs and long-term investing automatically.

Auto-mandate for full payment — discipline once vs. struggle monthly

Set an auto-mandate to pay the **full outstanding amount** from your Expense Account. Auto-mandate shifts discipline from a monthly decision to a one-time setup. A single missed full payment can undo years of progress.

Auto-mandate removes:

- Forgetfulness
- Emotional delay
- Minimum-due temptation

But: do a quick statement review before auto-pay executes, so errors or fraud do not go unnoticed.

If your Expense Account cannot support full auto-payment, the spending pattern needs correction — not a higher limit.

Lifetime-free cards and rewards — keep it simple

Choose simplicity. For most people, a lifetime-free card with straightforward benefits is better than a premium card with fees that force you to spend more to 'recover' the cost.

Rewards are nice. They are not a reason to buy. Treat rewards as incidental bonuses, not goals.

Avoid upgrading cards unless your spending pattern clearly justifies it — not because of marketing.

EMIs — convenience that deserves a plan

EMI conversions make big purchases feel lighter. But EMIs:

- Reduce future cash flow
- Crowd monthly budgets
- Delay investing consistency

Use EMIs only for essential, planned expenses — and only for short tenures. Never convert everyday consumption into long EMIs.

One-Page Credit Card Rules Checklist (pin this page)

Use this as your permanent rulebook. If any box is broken, suspend card use until discipline is restored.

Spending:

- I spend only what already exists in my Expense Account.
- I do not use the card to cover lifestyle gaps.
- I avoid impulse purchases, even if rewards exist.

Payment:

- I pay the full outstanding balance every month.
- Auto-mandate for full payment is active and linked to my Expense Account.
- I never rely on the minimum due.

Control:

- My credit limit aligns with discipline, not eligibility.
- I use one or two cards max; no overlapping cards.
- I review the statement monthly before auto-pay executes.

Behaviour:

- Rewards do not change my spending decisions.
- I avoid EMI conversions for wants.
- If any purchase feels uncomfortable after swiping, I pause card use.

Non-Negotiable Rule:

Never use a credit card for cash withdrawal.

Cash withdrawals carry immediate interest and fees — they break discipline instantly.

A calm self-check (use monthly)

Ask yourself:

- Did I pay the full bill this month?
- Did any purchase feel uncomfortable after swiping?
- Did credit card spending reduce investing capacity?

If any answer is "yes", pause and reset.

When credit cards truly help

They are useful when they:

- Smooth timing (booking, short delays)
- Build credit history via responsible use
- Add convenience without increasing spending

The moment they fund lifestyle inflation, they stop being helpful.

End-of-Chapter Summary

- Credit cards amplify behaviour — the right mindset prevents traps.
- Use the debit-card mindset: only spend what you can pay.
- Credit cards belong only to the Expense Account.
- Auto-mandate for full payment, but review statements monthly.
- Never withdraw cash on a credit card.
- Simple, lifetime-free cards with discipline beat premium cards without control.

One line to remember

Credit cards should support your life — never silently control it.

CHAPTER TWENTY

Monthly Investment Plans by Income Level — Start Small, Stay Consistent

There Is No Perfect Income to Begin

One of the biggest myths in investing is this:

"I will start investing properly once my income increases."

In reality, investing does not depend on how much you earn. It depends on how early and how consistently you start.

This chapter shows practical monthly investment plans for different income levels — low, medium, and higher — and explains what to do as your financial capacity improves.

The goal is not perfection. The goal is progress without pressure.

Before you begin — one non-negotiable rule

Before following any plan in this chapter:

- An emergency fund of at least **3–6 months of expenses** should be in place
- High-interest debt (credit cards, personal loans) should be under control

If this foundation is missing, investing will feel stressful instead of empowering.

Profile 1: Lower-Income Investor — discipline over amount

Example income: ₹15,000 – ₹30,000 per month

At this stage, survival and stability matter more than aggressive investing.

Suggested approach

- Investment amount: **5%–10% of income**
- Focus: **habit formation, not returns**

Where to invest

- One diversified equity mutual fund SIP
- Optional: small recurring deposit for stability

Even **₹500– ₹1,000 per month** is enough to begin building the habit.

The objective here is simple:

Teach your money to move towards the future every month.

Consistency matters more than comfort.

Why starting early matters more than amount

Many people believe big money creates big wealth.

Time tells a different story.

Simple truth:

Small money + long time beats big money + short time.

A simple comparison

Assuming an average long-term return of around **10–12% per year**, the early investor benefits significantly from compounding.

- Person A invests ₹2,000 per month from age 25 to 35 (10 years)
- Person B invests ₹5,000 per month from age 35 to 60 (25 years)

Despite investing less overall, Person A can end up with comparable — or sometimes even higher — wealth because **time does the heavy lifting.**

You may not control the amount you can invest today. But you can control **time and discipline.**

That is your advantage.

A simple real-world illustration:

Ramen, a delivery executive earning ₹18,000 per month, started a ₹500 SIP at age 24.

He increased it by ₹250 every year as his income improved.

By age 40, his investments had grown to over ₹7 lakh — even though many of his friends with higher salaries had still not started investing.

The lesson is simple:

Consistency and time quietly outperform income and intention.

The most important idea first — a simple compounding formula

You do not need complex calculations to understand compounding. Just remember this:

Small amount × Long time × Consistency = Wealth

Compounding is not magic. It is simply time doing work that effort cannot.

This formula works for everyone — **not just high earners.**

Profile 2: Middle-Income Investor — balance and growth

Example income: ₹30,000 – ₹75,000 per month

This phase allows both stability and growth.

Suggested approach

- Investment amount: **15%–25% of income**
- Focus: **balance between present and future**

Where to invest

- Equity mutual fund SIPs (core)
- Debt fund or RD for stability
- Term insurance and health insurance must be active

At this level:

- SIPs should be automated
- Investment account must stay protected

Lifestyle upgrades are allowed — but investing should upgrade first.

Profile 3: Higher-Income Investor — structure over complexity

Example income: ₹75,000+ per month

Higher income increases options — and also increases mistakes if structure is missing.

Suggested approach

- Investment amount: **25%–40% of income**
- Focus: **protection, diversification, tax efficiency**

Where to invest

- Multiple equity mutual funds (diversified)
- Debt instruments for stability
- Retirement-focused investments

Avoid the trap of complexity.
More products do not mean better results.
Clarity always beats cleverness.

A Quiet Example of What Consistency Looks Like

Namita started with a ₹1,500 SIP at 24. She increased it slowly whenever her salary increased. No shortcuts. No timing. No panic. By 40, her investments quietly crossed ₹30 lakh.

She never felt rich. But she never felt stressed either. That was her real return.

What to do after emergency fund is achieved

Once your emergency fund is complete:

- Redirect surplus money to SIPs
- Increase SIP amounts gradually
- Avoid sudden lifestyle inflation

A simple rule:
Increase investments first. Let lifestyle follow slowly.
This single habit creates long-term financial freedom.

How to increase investments safely

Instead of big jumps:

- Increase SIPs annually
- Use bonuses and increments wisely
- Avoid stopping SIPs during temporary stress

Small increases done regularly outperform dramatic changes done rarely.

Common mistakes across all income levels

- Waiting for the "right" income
- Starting too many investments at once
- Copying others without personal context
- Stopping SIPs for short-term reasons
- Treating investing as optional

Wealth is built through **boring consistency, not exciting decisions.**

End-of-Chapter Summary

- There is no minimum income required to start investing
- Early start matters more than big amounts
- Investment percentage should rise with income
- Emergency fund comes first, always
- Discipline compounds faster than money

One line to remember

You don't build wealth by waiting for more money — you build it by starting with what you have.

CHAPTER TWENTY-ONE

Investing Mistakes That Steal Time, Not Just Money

Anchor idea

Most investors don't lose money in the market.
They lose time outside the market.

The cost nobody calculates

When people talk about investing mistakes, they usually talk about money lost.

But the most damaging investing mistakes do not show up immediately in rupees. They show up years later — when compounding should have been working, but wasn't.

Money can be earned again. Time cannot.

This chapter is not about market crashes or bad products. It is about silent behaviours that quietly steal years of compounding — even from disciplined investors.

The most dangerous mistake — starting and stopping

Nothing harms compounding more than interruption.

Many investors:

- Start SIPs with enthusiasm
- Stop during fear or uncertainty
- Restart later with regret

Every stop resets momentum. Compounding works quietly in the background.

Think of compounding like a train. Missing one month doesn't stop the train — but repeatedly stepping off delays arrival by years.

Compounding does not pause politely — it resets.

Missing a few strong market years can undo a decade of effort. Consistency, not brilliance, creates long-term results.

Waiting for certainty before acting

Common thoughts sound reasonable:

- Markets are too high right now
- I'll start when income improves
- I need more clarity first

But markets are never certain. Income is never fully stable. Clarity comes from action — not delay.

Waiting feels safe, but it silently steals time.

Most people don't regret investing too early. They regret waiting too long.

An investor who waits five extra years to begin investing often has to invest two to three times more every month later just to catch up.

A Familiar Pattern — and its Hidden Cost

Ram stopped investing after a market crash. For three years, he stayed out, waiting for stability.

When he finally returned, the market had already recovered.

He didn't lose money. He lost time. And in investing, lost time is rarely recovered easily.

This time, he chose consistency over fear. And slowly, time started working for him again.

Over-monitoring and emotional interference

Checking portfolios daily creates noise, not insight.

Constant exposure to:

- News headlines
- Social media opinions
- WhatsApp tips

turns investing into emotional work.
Compounding needs boredom. Attention breaks patience.

Breaking long-term investments for short-term comfort

Using future money for present convenience is a common mistake.
Examples include:

- Breaking retirement funds for lifestyle needs
- Using investments as backup savings
- Treating long-term goals casually

Once broken, compounding does not resume from the same point. Restarting later always costs more time and effort.

Chasing "better" instead of staying invested

Many investors constantly search for:

- Better funds
- Better strategies
- Better returns

This leads to:

- Frequent switching
- Product hopping
- Loss of continuity

Good investments held consistently outperform perfect choices interrupted repeatedly.

Ignoring life changes — or overreacting to them

Two extremes damage progress:

1. Never adjusting investments as life evolves
2. Changing everything due to short-term events

The correct approach is balance.
Adjust structure as life changes. Do not change behaviour emotionally.
Annual review is discipline. Constant reaction is damage.

Confusing complexity with progress

More apps. More funds. More strategies.
Complexity increases friction. Friction reduces consistency.
Simple systems survive stress. Complicated systems break quietly.

A Short Real-Life Contrast — Same Income, Different Time Use

Two people earn similar incomes.
One invests steadily, rarely changes plans, and ignores noise.
The other reacts, optimizes, pauses, and restarts.
Years later, the difference is not intelligence or income.
It is uninterrupted time.
And over long periods, uninterrupted time creates results that effort alone cannot.

The Quiet Advantage of Staying Invested

Ripon started investing with a small SIP in his late twenties.
There were market ups and downs, news cycles, and moments of doubt — but he followed one simple rule:

He did not stop.

He did not try to time the market. He did not pause during uncertainty. He did not chase better options every year.

He simply continued.

Over the years, nothing dramatic happened. No sudden windfall. No exciting shortcuts.

But something more powerful happened quietly.

Time kept working.

While others stopped and restarted, Ripon stayed invested — and that uninterrupted time created a gap that kept widening.

His returns did not come from perfect decisions.

They came from decisions he did not interrupt.

The quiet rule that protects compounding

Remember this rule:

Anything that interrupts consistency steals compounding.

Volatility does not destroy wealth. Interrupted discipline does.

A bridge to the next part — protecting time through habits

The solution is not prediction. It is structure.

Systems beat willpower. Habits beat motivation.

The next part of this book focuses on money habits that protect time — and allow wealth to multiply quietly.

End-of-Chapter Summary

- Time is the real investment asset
- Most damage is behavioural, not technical
- Consistency matters more than optimisation
- Avoid interruptions, not volatility

One line to remember

Your future wealth is not built by perfect decisions. It is built by decisions you didn't interrupt.

Money Habits That Protect & Multiply Wealth (Your Edge)

Wealth is rarely lost suddenly

Most people do not lose money because they make one terrible decision.

They lose it quietly.

Through small habits. Through ignored warnings. Through decisions that feel harmless in the moment.

By now, you have learned how to:

- Earn and structure money
- Start investing calmly
- Build systems that work automatically
- Avoid major mistakes that destroy progress

Yet there is one uncomfortable truth to understand:

Knowing what to do does not guarantee long-term success.

Behaviour, not knowledge, decides financial outcomes.

Many people know what to do with money. Very few behave consistently enough to benefit from it.

Up to now, you have built systems. From here onward, you will learn how to **protect them.**

Investments create returns. **Habits protect those returns.**

Without the right money habits:

- Even good investments get interrupted.
- Compounding gets broken
- Discipline collapses during stress

This is why many intelligent people stay financially stuck — not because they choose wrong products, but because their daily money behaviour quietly works against long-term growth.

Wealth is destroyed by behaviour, not by lack of knowledge

Wealth is rarely destroyed by one bad decision. It is destroyed by **unnoticed repetition**.

You do not make one financial decision in life. You make thousands of small ones:

- How you use credit
- How you take loans
- How you react during market fear
- How you spend after income increases
- How you behave when life becomes unpredictable

These behaviours repeat quietly. Over time, they either:

- Protect compounding
- Or leak compounding

This part of the book focuses on habits — not numbers. Because habits decide whether compounding works for you or against you.

Protection before multiplication

Most books focus on how to make more money. Very few focus on how to **not lose the progress you've already made.**

In this part, you will learn:

- How to distinguish good loans from bad loans
- How to use leverage without losing control
- How to avoid lifestyle traps after income growth
- How to stay invested during fear, boredom, and overconfidence

These habits act like financial shock absorbers. They keep your journey smooth even when life throws bumps.

Who this part is especially for

This part is for you if:

- You already invest but feel progress is slow
- You earn better now but feel less calm
- You fear one mistake could undo years of effort
- You want wealth to feel stable — not stressful

You do not need advanced strategies. You need behavioural clarity.

How to read this part

Do not rush. Do not skim.

These chapters are not about information. They are about awareness, alignment, and restraint.

One corrected habit here can quietly save **years** of effort later.

One idea to carry forward

Investments grow money. Habits protect time.

Wealth needs both.

Let's build the habits that quietly **protect — and then multiply —** everything you've already started.

CHAPTER TWENTY-TWO

Lifestyle Inflation — The Silent Enemy of Progress

The invisible leak

Most people do not fail financially because they earn too little. They fail because their expenses quietly rise to match their income.

Lifestyle inflation rarely feels dangerous — it feels deserved and justified. A better phone. A bigger house. A costlier car. More conveniences.

None of these feel like mistakes. That is why lifestyle inflation is so powerful.

This chapter explains how financial progress is often undone *after* success — not before it.

What lifestyle inflation really is (and what it isn't)

Lifestyle inflation is not about enjoying life less. It is not about living cheaply forever. Lifestyle inflation is **automatic upgrading without intention**. It happens slowly, often without noticing.

Examples:

- Expenses increasing simply because income increased
- EMIs added because they "fit the salary"
- Subscriptions and comforts that never scale down
- Fixed costs rising faster than investments

Important distinction:
Conscious upgrades are healthy. Unconscious inflation is dangerous.

Why lifestyle inflation feels harmless

Lifestyle inflation hides behind logic:

- I can afford it now
- Everyone at my level does this
- I deserve this upgrade

Each decision feels reasonable. But together, they create a fragile financial structure.

The danger is not one upgrade. The danger is **many permanent upgrades made without planning**. Each one seems small, but together they quietly reshape your financial future.

A Simple Example — When Income Grows Faster than Discipline

When Ankit received his first big salary raise, he upgraded everything.

A bigger apartment. A new car. A more expensive phone.

Each decision felt justified. His income had increased, and the upgrades felt like progress.

But over time, something changed. His income doubled — yet his savings barely improved.

His colleague, Ritu, made a different choice.

When her salary increased, she increased her investments first. Her lifestyle improved too — but slowly, and with intention.

Ten years later, their financial lives looked completely different.

Lesson:

Income growth does not build wealth.
What you do with that growth does.

The real cost — time, not money

Lifestyle inflation does not just reduce savings. It delays freedom.

A ₹10,000 monthly lifestyle upgrade can:

- Reduce long-term investments by lakhs

- Increase dependency on income
- Add pressure during emergencies
- Steal years of optional work and peace

Money can often be earned again; time usually cannot. **Time lost to broken compounding cannot be recovered.**

Why income growth makes this problem worse

As income rises:

- Stakes increase
- EMIs become larger
- Fixed costs become heavier
- Mistakes become expensive

A small habit at ₹25,000 income is recoverable. The same habit at ₹ 1,00,000 income is damaging.

Lifestyle discipline is not only for beginners. It is essential for people who are doing well.

The upgrade order that protects wealth

To avoid lifestyle inflation, upgrades must follow a simple order:

1. Protection first

- Emergency fund
- Insurance

2. Investments second

- SIP increases
- Long-term goals

3. Lifestyle last

- Conscious, planned upgrades

If lifestyle upgrades come first, progress stays fragile.

Lifestyle inflation vs. Lifestyle improvement

Not all spending is bad.

The difference lies in intention.

Lifestyle inflation:

- Emotion-driven
- Permanent expense
- Reduces flexibility

Lifestyle improvement:

- Value-driven
- Planned and affordable
- Does not break investing systems

A simple self-check:

"Does this upgrade increase my calm — or increase my pressure?"

Simple rules to control lifestyle inflation

You do not need complex budgeting. You need a few boring rules:

- Increase investments **before** increasing lifestyle
- Lock SIP increases to income hikes
- Treat bonuses as future money, not spending money
- Avoid EMIs for wants
- Delay major upgrades by 30–60 days

Boring rules protect exciting futures.

Why this habit compounds quietly

When expenses grow slowly:

- Savings increase naturally

- Stress reduces
- Investment discipline strengthens
- Flexibility improves

Lifestyle control does not restrict life in the long run. It **buys options.** Options create freedom.

A quiet reminder about progress

A senior colleague once shared a simple observation.

"In the early years, every salary increase feels like a reward. It feels natural to upgrade life along with it."

He paused for a moment and then added,

"But the people who quietly moved ahead were not the ones who upgraded fastest. They were the ones who created a gap — between what they earned and what they spent — and protected that gap."

Lifestyle upgrades feel visible. Progress does not.

But over time, that invisible gap becomes freedom.

Final Thought

Wealth is not built by how much your lifestyle grows.
It is built by how much you choose not to upgrade.

End-of-Chapter Summary

- Lifestyle inflation is silent, not dramatic
- It steals time more than money
- Income growth without discipline delays freedom
- Investments must upgrade before lifestyle
- Wealth grows fastest when expenses grow slowly

One line to remember

Your lifestyle should rise slower than your income — that gap is where freedom is built.

CHAPTER TWENTY-THREE

Good Loans vs. Bad Loans — A Behavioural Guide to Borrowing Safely

Loans don't create problems, behaviour does

Loans are not evil. Avoiding all loans is not wisdom.

Loans are tools, not enemies — used carefully, they can support growth; used carelessly, they can quietly hurt you.

But borrowing without intention is dangerous.

Loans amplify behaviour. If habits are disciplined, loans can support growth. If habits are emotional, loans quietly destroy years of progress.

The real danger is not borrowing money. The real danger is borrowing without understanding what the loan is doing to your future.

This chapter will help you see loans clearly — not as numbers, but as behavioural decisions.

Why people get loans wrong (the behavioural traps)

Most people do not misuse loans because they are careless. They misuse loans because of psychological shortcuts.

Common traps:

- Focusing on EMI instead of total cost
- Replacing affordability with "I can manage the EMI"
- Normalising long-term EMIs for short-term comfort

- Borrowing more as income increases
- Treating loans as lifestyle enablers instead of tools

A ₹40,000 EMI can feel "manageable" — but over 20 years, it may cost several lakhs in interest.

Loans fail people mentally before they fail financially.

Asset-creating loans vs. Liability-creating loans (the core distinction)

Not all loans are equal.

The simplest way to judge a loan is this:

Does this loan improve my future capacity — or reduce it?

Asset-creating loans

These loans help you earn more, grow skills, or build stability.

Examples:

- Education loan that leads to employable skills
- Business loan with predictable cash flow
- Reasonable home loan for long-term shelter

These loans are not "good" automatically. They are useful only when controlled.

Liability-creating loans

These loans fund consumption — not capacity.

Examples:

- Personal loans for lifestyle
- Long-term EMIs for gadgets and travel
- Credit card balances rolled forward
- Loans used to maintain appearances

If a loan does not improve your future earning ability or stability, it is almost always a liability.

Loans that can help build wealth (used carefully)

Some loans can coexist with wealth-building — if discipline stays intact.

Home loan (within limits)

- EMI should not dominate income
- SIPs must continue
- Lifestyle should not inflate alongside EMI

Education loan

- Skill must have earning clarity
- Repayment should feel predictable
- Lifestyle should remain modest initially

Business loan

- Cash flow must support EMI
- Borrowing must expand capacity, not cover losses

A powerful rule:
If SIPs stop because of a loan, the loan is too heavy.

Loans that quietly destroy investments

Some loans look harmless — but are extremely damaging.

- Personal loans for convenience
- Lifestyle EMIs stretched over years
- Credit card rollovers and minimum dues
- Borrowing to maintain lifestyle during income gaps

These loans:

- Reduce future cash flow
- Crowd out investing
- Increase stress during downturns

- Break compounding silently

Warning sign:

If your investments exist only when income is high, the loan structure is weak.

How loans should coexist with investing

Healthy borrowing follows clear rules:

- SIPs continue during loan repayment
- EMIs and investments fit calmly within income
- Loans do not replace saving behavior
- Borrowing never becomes a lifestyle substitute

Borrowing and investing must move together, not compete.
If one kills the other, the structure is fragile.

When borrowing becomes unavoidable (emergencies)

Some situations force borrowing:

- Medical emergencies
- Job loss or business disruption

In such cases:

- Borrow only what is necessary
- Avoid lifestyle maintenance loans
- Exit the loan as early as possible

Emergency loans are recovery tools — not financial strategies.

A quick borrowing self-check (before taking any loan)

Before signing any loan, pause and ask:

- Does this loan improve future income or stability?
- Will my SIPs continue comfortably?
- Can I repay even if income slows?
- Am I borrowing for value — or emotion?

If answers feel unclear, delay the loan.
Clarity saves years.

End-of-Chapter Summary

- Loans amplify behavior
- EMIs can hide long-term damage
- Asset loans build capacity; liability loans steal time
- Investments must survive loan periods
- Safe borrowing protects compounding

One line to remember

A good loan supports your future. A bad loan steals it quietly.

CHAPTER TWENTY-FOUR

Using Investments Smartly in Emergencies (Without Breaking Your Future)

Emergencies test behaviour, not knowledge

Emergencies do not announce themselves. They arrive suddenly — medical issues, job disruptions, family responsibilities, unexpected repairs.

What decides long-term outcomes is not the emergency itself. It is how you respond in the first few moments.

Panic creates permanent damage. Calm structure limits the damage.

This chapter is not about avoiding emergencies. It is about choosing the least harmful financial response when emergencies occur.

Why emergencies destroy wealth more than bad investments

Most long-term wealth damage does not come from choosing the wrong mutual fund. It comes from emergency reactions.

Common damage during emergencies:

- Forced selling of long-term investments
- Taking high-interest debt in panic
- Breaking disciplined systems built over years
- Turning temporary problems into permanent setbacks

A bad investment can recover with time. A broken compounding cycle often cannot.

Example:
During the 2020 pandemic, many investors sold equity mutual funds in panic to cover temporary income loss. Within two years, markets recovered sharply — but those who sold had already locked in losses and missed the recovery.

The Emergency Decision Ladder — choose before panic

When emergencies strike, decisions must follow a hierarchy.
Jumping steps creates unnecessary damage.

Think of it as a financial ladder — always climb from the safest step first.

Always climb from the top. Never jump levels emotionally.

Level 1 — Emergency fund (first line of defence)

This is why emergency funds exist.

- Savings account or liquid fund
- No interest cost
- No compounding damage
- No repayment stress

If an emergency fund is available, use it without guilt. This is not failure — this is preparation working.

Level 2 — Reduce the shock before borrowing

Before borrowing or selling anything:

- Pause non-essential spending
- Delay lifestyle payments
- Cancel or freeze optional expenses
- Use short-term flexibility

Often, this step alone reduces the required amount significantly. Smaller problems need smaller solutions.

Level 3 — Borrowing against safety nets (lower damage options)

If emergency funds are insufficient, the next layer is rule-based borrowing.

EPF/PPF loans

- Interest is lower than personal loans
- Access is limited (protective friction)
- Designed for genuine emergencies

Rules for using EPF/PPF loans:

- Use only as a temporary bridge
- Avoid recurring usage
- Plan exit early

Retirement money may bend in emergencies — but it should never break permanently.

Level 4 — Borrowing against investments (with discipline)

Instead of selling investments, borrowing against them can sometimes cause less long-term damage.

Loan against mutual funds or stocks

- Interest rates are lower than personal loans
- Investments remain invested
- Compounding continues if markets recover

Important discipline rules:

- Borrow only a portion of the portfolio
- Avoid borrowing during extreme market volatility
- Ensure EMI fits comfortably within income

- Exit the loan as early as possible

Borrowing against investments is not free money. It is a controlled compromise — safer than panic selling, but still temporary.

Level 5 — Last-resort borrowing (high-damage zone)

This includes:

- Personal loans
- Credit card rollovers
- App-based instant loans

Characteristics:

- High interest
- Emotional stress
- Long recovery periods

These options should be used only when survival is at risk. Never for lifestyle maintenance.

Why selling investments should be the last emotional choice

Selling investments during emergencies:

- Locks losses permanently
- Restarts the compounding clock
- Creates regret during recovery

Selling is not always wrong. Panic selling is almost always wrong.

Selling vs. Borrowing — how to decide calmly

The goal is simple: choose the option that causes the least long-term damage to your financial future.

Ask yourself:

- Is this emergency temporary or long-term?
- Can I handle EMIs calmly if income slows?
- Will I regret selling this investment in five years?

Choose the option that protects future flexibility, not present comfort.

Red flags that signal weak emergency structure

- Frequent borrowing
- Repeated investment withdrawals
- Emergencies becoming lifestyle support

These are planning gaps — not income problems.

How to rebuild after an emergency

Once stability returns:

- Rebuild emergency fund first
- Close emergency loans early
- Restart SIPs immediately
- Review protection gaps

Recovery speed matters more than recovery pride.

Final Thought — Wealth Is Quiet

Financial planning is not about predicting every problem. Life will always bring surprises. The goal is not perfection — it is preparation.

When difficult moments arrive, calm structure protects what years of discipline have built.

Wealth is not defined by how fast it grows, but by how well it survives difficult moments.

Quiet discipline today becomes financial freedom tomorrow.

Wealth grows quietly. Protect it patiently.

End-of-Chapter Summary

- Emergencies require hierarchy, not panic
- Emergency funds come first
- EPF/PPF and investment-backed loans are safer bridges
- High-interest debt causes long-term damage
- Compounding must be protected even during crises

One line to remember

In emergencies, aim for survival with minimum future damage — not comfort today.

CHAPTER TWENTY-FIVE

Rent First, Buy Home Later — Why Rushing to Buy Can Delay Wealth

The most emotional financial decision

Buying a home is not just a financial decision in India. It is a social milestone.

Family pressure. Social respect. Emotional security. "Own house" is treated as proof of success.

Because of this, many people buy homes before they are financially ready — not because it is optimal, but because it feels necessary.

This chapter is not anti-homeownership. It is anti-haste.

The common belief — rent is wasted money

Most people grow up hearing:

- Rent is wasted
- EMI is better than rent
- At least you own something

This belief sounds logical — but it is incomplete.

Rent is not wasted if it buys flexibility and time to grow. EMI is not smart if it kills investing and peace.

The real question is not rent vs buy. The real question is timing.

What rushing into a home actually costs

When people buy a home too early, three things usually happen together:

- Large EMI starts
- SIPs slow down or stop
- Lifestyle pressure increases

The damage is subtle, not immediate.
For years, it looks like progress. But wealth quietly delays.
A home bought early often consumes:

- Future salary hikes
- Bonus money
- Emergency buffers
- Investment discipline

You may own a house — yet remain financially tight for years.

Rent + invest — the invisible advantage

Renting early in life offers something powerful: optionality.
Renting allows you to:

- Keep EMIs zero or low
- Invest aggressively
- Change cities or jobs freely
- Handle emergencies calmly

Money that would have gone into EMI goes into early-stage compounding, where time matters most.
This advantage is invisible in year one. It becomes obvious in year ten.

A simple comparison (illustrative, not perfect)

Consider two people, both earning ₹60,000 per month.

Person A — buys early

- Home loan EMI: ₹25,000
- SIP: ₹5,000

Person B — rents

- Rent: ₹12,000
- SIP: ₹18,000

Both spend similar amounts monthly. But the direction of money is different.

After 10–12 years:

- Person A owns a partially paid house
- Person B owns a growing investment portfolio

Person B now has:

- Stronger down-payment power
- Negotiation strength
- Choice

Timing created the gap.

This example is simplified to illustrate the behavioural difference. Actual outcomes will depend on market returns, property prices, and personal discipline.

When renting is financially smarter

Renting makes sense when:

- Income is still rising
- Career is flexible or unstable

- City may change
- Emergency fund is not solid
- SIP discipline is more important than ownership

Renting is not weakness. It is strategic patience.

When buying a home makes sense

Buying becomes sensible when:

- Income is stable and predictable
- Emergency fund is fully ready
- SIPs continue comfortably after EMI
- Down payment does not drain all savings
- Location and lifestyle are settled
- Schooling, family stability, or long-term location certainty exists

A good home purchase should add calm, not anxiety.

A house should become security, not stress.

Timing matters as much as ownership.

If buying increases stress, the timing is wrong.

The EMI illusion — "rent equals EMI"

The "rent equals EMI" argument ignores several ownership costs that appear only after buying.

Many people justify buying by saying:

"My rent is already equal to EMI."

This ignores hidden costs:

- Maintenance
- Property tax
- Repairs
- Registration and stamp duty
- Reduced flexibility

EMI is not the full cost of ownership. Rent is not the full cost of renting.

Always compare total impact, not just monthly numbers.

Home is not an investment — it is shelter first

A self-occupied home is primarily:

- Shelter
- Stability
- Emotional security

Treating it as a wealth engine creates pressure.
Homes can appreciate — but slowly, unevenly, and with illiquidity.
Your financial freedom comes from cash-flowing assets, not walls.
Buy a home for life. Build wealth elsewhere.

A calm rule to follow

Before buying a home, ask:

- Will my SIPs survive this EMI?
- Can I handle this loan if income slows?
- Am I buying from clarity or pressure?

If answers are uncertain, renting longer is not failure. It is preparation.

End-of-Chapter Summary

- Buying a home is emotional, timing is financial
- Rushing into ownership often delays wealth
- Renting early can accelerate investing
- Buy when stability exists, not when pressure peaks
- A good home adds peace, not financial strain

One line to remember

Rent buys time. Time builds wealth. Buy only when time is on your side.

CHAPTER TWENTY-SIX

Rent vs. Buy — Smarter Choices for Luxury Gadgets & Modern Living

Ownership is no longer the default

There was a time when owning things was necessary. If you needed something, you bought it. Access without ownership was rare.

Today, that world has changed. Technology evolves faster than our ability to use it fully. Lifestyle products upgrade faster than our income stabilises.

Yet our mindset is still stuck in an older rule:

"If I can afford it, I should own it."

This chapter is not about denying comfort. It is about understanding when ownership builds value — and when it quietly destroys it.

The ownership trap — why buying feels safer than renting

Ownership feels secure.

When you own something:

- It feels permanent
- It feels controlled
- It feels like progress

Renting or temporary access often feels inferior, even when it is financially smarter.

This emotional bias pushes people to buy:

- Expensive gadgets "just in case"
- Appliances used a few times a year
- High-end upgrades driven more by convenience than necessity.

The problem is not the purchase itself.

The problem is buying to feel settled, not because it is financially sensible.

Ownership often buys emotional comfort — not actual value.

What depreciates fastest (and why it matters)

Some things lose value slowly. Some lose value the moment you buy them.

Fast-depreciating items usually share three traits:

- Technology changes quickly
- New versions appear frequently
- Resale value is poor in real life

Luxury gadgets, electronics, and lifestyle tech fall into this category.

Money locked into these items:

- Cannot compound
- Cannot be redeployed
- Quietly exits your wealth system

You are not just paying money. You are paying opportunity cost. Money saved from unnecessary ownership can instead be invested where it compounds for years.

A Simple Real-Life Example — the Expensive Camera Lens

Consider a photography enthusiast who buys a high-end camera lens for ₹ 2,50,000.

It feels like a professional upgrade.

In reality:

- It is used for 2–3 trips a year
- Newer versions appear within a few years
- Resale value drops sharply

That ₹2.5 lakh remains locked in a cupboard for most of the year.

The same lens could be rented for a few thousand rupees per trip — while the remaining capital stays invested and compounding.

The difference is not photography quality.

The difference is simple: whether your capital works for you — or sits idle.

When renting or accessing makes more sense

Renting or accessing is financially smarter when:

- Usage is occasional, not daily
- The need is temporary
- Technology evolves rapidly
- The purchase is convenience-driven, not income-driven

Examples include:

- Short-term lifestyle upgrades
- Rarely used equipment
- High-end gadgets bought for novelty
- One-time personal or family requirements

In these cases, ownership does not create advantage. It creates friction. Access gives flexibility. Flexibility protects capital.

Rent vs. Buy — the comparison most people miss

Most people compare:

- Rent amount vs. purchase price
- Monthly payment vs. EMI

This is the wrong comparison.
The correct comparison is:

- Capital locked vs. capital available

Buying locks money. Renting preserves liquidity.
Liquidity allows:

- Investing
- Emergency handling
- Career flexibility
- Calm decision-making

Renting is not cheaper in the short term. It is more powerful in the long-term when it protects investable capital.

Emotional justifications — and what they hide

Common justifications sound reasonable:

- I'll use it a lot
- It saves time
- It improves productivity

But few people actually measure:

- Usage frequency after novelty fades
- Productivity improvement over months
- Opportunity cost of blocked capital

Many purchases are justified once — but paid for silently for years.

Smart access rules — so renting doesn't become lifestyle inflation

Renting smartly does not mean consuming endlessly.

Rules that protect wealth:

- Rent only what you genuinely need
- Avoid upgrading just because access is easy
- Treat rental spending like ownership spending — with limits
- Never replace investment discipline with convenience

Access is a tool. Without discipline, it becomes another spending trap.

When buying actually makes sense

Ownership is still powerful when:

- Usage is frequent and long-term
- Replacement cycles are slow
- The item improves earning capacity
- Cost is a small portion of net worth

Buying is sensible when ownership reduces long-term friction, not increases it.

This book is not anti-buy. It is pro-intentionality.

The real behavioural shift

Modern wealth is not built by owning more things.

It is built by:

- Owning assets
- Accessing conveniences
- Protecting liquidity
- Letting money compound quietly

Objects age. Capital grows.

Choose accordingly.

To make this idea practical, it helps to understand when renting or buying usually makes more sense in everyday decisions.

When Renting Makes Financial Sense

Renting often makes sense when:

- The product becomes outdated quickly
- You use it only occasionally
- Maintenance costs are high
- A newer version appears frequently

Examples include:

- DSLR or mirror-less cameras for hobby use
- Projectors
- High-end gaming consoles
- Drones for occasional photography
- Party equipment
- Camping equipment used once or twice a year
- Power tools needed for occasional repairs

In these situations, paying only for temporary use can be more efficient than owning.

When Buying Is the Better Choice

Buying makes more sense when:

- The product is used daily
- It has a long lifespan
- Renting costs accumulate quickly
- Maintenance is simple

Examples include:

- Refrigerator

- Washing machine
- Laptop for work

In these cases, ownership provides convenience and long-term value.

Smart financial decisions are not about owning more things. They are about owning the right things for the right reasons.

End-of-Chapter Summary

- Ownership feels safe, but often blocks capital
- Fast-depreciating items damage compounding
- Renting preserves liquidity and flexibility
- Access must be disciplined, not impulsive
- Own assets — access comforts

One line to remember

Own what grows your wealth. Access what fades with time.

All examples in this chapter are simplified to illustrate behavioural concepts. Actual outcomes will vary depending on market returns, interest rates, product lifespans, and personal discipline.

CHAPTER TWENTY-SEVEN

Subscription Audit — Stop Paying for What You Don't Use

The smallest leaks sink the fastest

Most people believe wealth leaks happen through big mistakes. A bad investment. A wrong loan. A failed business idea.

In reality, some of the biggest financial damage happens quietly — through small, ignored monthly payments.

₹199 here. ₹299 there. ₹499 auto-debited without thought. Subscriptions rarely feel painful. That is exactly why they are dangerous.

Wealth rarely leaks in large chunks. It leaks through small amounts that repeat without attention.

Why subscriptions are more dangerous than big expenses

Big expenses create awareness.

- EMIs feel heavy
- Large purchases trigger discussion
- Loans demand planning

Subscriptions do the opposite.

- They are small

- They are automatic
- They fade into the background

Once activated, they no longer feel like decisions. They become habits.

Auto-debit removes friction. And when friction disappears, awareness disappears too.

Most people do not choose their subscriptions every month. They simply forget to stop them.

The modern subscription trap (today's reality)

Modern life is built on subscriptions.

Common examples include:

- OTT platforms (often multiple, overlapping)
- Music and cloud storage
- Fitness apps and memberships
- Food delivery and convenience plans
- Learning apps, tools, newsletters
- Bank add-ons, card protection plans

Annual "convenience plans" on food delivery or shopping apps often continue long after actual usage drops.

Each one seems reasonable in isolation. Together, they quietly consume investable money.

The real problem is not subscribing. The problem is never reviewing.

Most subscriptions survive not because they are valuable — but because cancellation keeps getting postponed.

Why free trials become permanent

Free trials remove the most important financial barrier — the moment of decision.

Once the trial converts into auto-payment, cancellation becomes a future task.

And future tasks are often ignored.

Many subscriptions survive not because they are valuable, but because they are easy to forget.

The real cost — not monthly, but permanent

The danger of subscriptions is not the amount. It is the permanence.

₹999 per month does not feel expensive, but it permanently reduces what you can invest.

A subscription is not a **one-time cost**. It is a standing instruction against your future wealth. The real cost becomes visible only when time enters the equation.

Example:

A ₹499 monthly subscription seems harmless. But ₹499 invested every month for 25 years at 12% annual returns could grow to more than ₹8–9 lakh.

Small payments repeated for decades quietly reshape financial futures — not because they are large, but because they are permanent.

That money could have:

- Increased SIPs
- Strengthened emergency buffers
- Reduced stress during income gaps

Subscriptions don't damage budgets. They damage long-term compounding capacity.

Subscription vs. Value — the clarity test

Before keeping any subscription, ask:

- When did I last use this fully?
- Would I subscribe again today at full price?
- Does this improve my health, income, or peace?
- Is this genuine value — or just convenience?

If the answer feels unclear, that is already an answer.

Unused subscriptions are not services. They are silent expenses.

Subscriptions should earn their place every few months. Silence is not approval.

The subscription audit — a 30-minute wealth habit

You do not need complex tracking. You need one honest review.

Step 1: List all auto-debits

- Bank accounts, cards and **UPI AutoPay mandates.**

Step 2: Categorise

- Essential • Optional • Forgotten

Step 3: Cancel aggressively

- Everything forgotten goes first.

Step 4: Review optional subscriptions quarterly

- If usage has faded, let it go.

This is not extreme. It is maintenance — like cleaning your financial house.

Redirecting waste into wealth (the habit shift)

The most important rule:

Cancelled subscriptions should not become extra spending money.

They should become automatic investment increases.

One cancelled ₹499 subscription, redirected into an SIP, quietly works for decades.

The habit matters more than the amount.

Stopping leakage is good. Redirecting savings is powerful.

How subscriptions quietly fuel lifestyle inflation

As income grows, subscriptions multiply.

- Another platform
- Another convenience

- Another "small" comfort

Life feels the same. But savings quietly shrink.
This is **lifestyle inflation running on autopilot.**
You don't feel richer. You just feel busier — with less flexibility.

Rules to keep subscriptions under control

Simple rules work best:

- No subscription without a review date
- No overlapping services serving the same purpose
- Annual audit is non-negotiable
- Annual plans only after proven usage
- Convenience should never replace discipline

Subscriptions are tools. Without limits, they become leaks.

When subscriptions are worth paying for

Not all subscriptions are bad.
They are worth paying for when they:

- Improve health consistently
- Increase earning ability
- Save meaningful time every week
- Reduce stress without increasing dependency

Pay freely for what compounds your life. Be strict with what only entertains it.

By now, you know what to do.
The final step is simple — staying consistent when it matters most.

Because in the end, it is not knowledge that builds wealth — it is what you do consistently.

End-of-Chapter Summary

- Subscriptions cause silent, long-term leakage
- Auto-debit reduces awareness and discipline
- Small amounts permanently reduce investing ability
- Regular audits protect future compounding
- Redirecting savings matters more than cancelling

One line to remember

What you stop paying for quietly decides what you can afford in the future.

CHAPTER TWENTY-EIGHT

Increase Income Early — Grow Skills While Time Is on Your Side

One of the biggest wealth mistakes is ignoring potential

Many young people focus only on surviving each month. Bills, responsibilities, and pressure feel immediate, so they work hard and hope income rises naturally with time.

Sometimes it does.

But one of the biggest wealth mistakes is quietly ignoring a stronger opportunity during these years:

Increasing your ability to earn.

The income you earn today matters. The income you can grow into may matter even more.

When people are young, they often have advantages that may become harder to use later:

- More energy
- Faster learning ability
- Greater flexibility
- Fewer financial responsibilities
- More willingness to adapt
- More time for future compounding

This chapter is not about chasing money endlessly.

It is about recognising a simple truth:

Your prime years are often the best years to grow skills that can raise income for decades.

Used wisely, that advantage can change your financial future.

Why skill growth matters more than many people realise

Income does not usually rise by hope alone. It often rises because value rises.

When you become better at solving problems, using tools, communicating clearly, leading people, or producing stronger results, your earning potential can improve.

Many people wait for income growth to happen automatically. Others actively build it.

That difference matters.

Two people may start at similar salaries. Over time, the person who keeps learning often creates wider opportunities.

Wealth is not built only by investing money. It is also built by increasing the amount available to invest.

Your current job may already contain the next opportunity

Many people look outside before improving inside.

They search for side income, business ideas, or dramatic career changes while ignoring the simplest path:

Becoming more valuable in the work they already do.

Examples:

- An office employee learns advanced spreadsheets, reporting, or automation
- A technician learns newer machines, software, or diagnostic tools
- A salesperson improves communication and customer trust
- A teacher learns digital teaching tools or new subject expertise
- A shop owner learns online selling, inventory systems, or digital marketing

Often the next income increase begins with better performance in the current role.

Do not underestimate small improvements repeated consistently.

Technology rewards learners

Every generation faces change.

Today, technology changes faster than before. New software, automation, digital systems, and artificial intelligence are reshaping many jobs.

Some people feel nervous when work begins to change. Others become curious and learn how to use new tools wisely.

Over time, curiosity is often rewarded.

Technology may replace some tasks. It also increases the value of people who can work effectively with it.

Learning modern tools can help you:

- Save time
- Improve output
- Solve problems faster
- Become more useful at work
- Stay relevant as industries change

The goal is not to chase every trend.

The goal is to remain adaptable.

A Simple Contrast — Same Age, Different Habits

Consider two friends in their twenties: Atul and Rohan.

Both started with similar salaries. Both worked sincerely. Both wanted a better future. Both were sincere. Neither imagined their choices would slowly separate their paths.

Atul believed experience alone would increase income with time.

Rohan believed experience mattered too — but kept learning alongside work.

He improved:

- Communication

- New tools
- Industry knowledge
- Productivity skills
- Professional confidence

Five years later, both had worked hard.

Neither had been lazy. But one had grown faster than the other.

Both gained experience. Only one turned experience into higher opportunity.

Often the income gap begins quietly long before it becomes visible.

Many people compare salaries. Few compare progress.

Small learning habits can create large financial outcomes

Many people imagine growth requires extreme sacrifice.

Usually it begins smaller:

- One useful course completed properly
- One new software skill learned well
- One certification with clear value
- Better writing or speaking ability
- Better understanding of your industry
- Learning how strong performers work

A few hours each week invested in capability can produce returns for years.

Money compounds.

Useful skills can compound too.

Do not wait for the perfect moment

Some people delay learning because life feels busy.

That feeling is real.

After office hours, energy can feel low. Weekends disappear quickly. Family responsibilities grow.

But later often becomes busier.

Responsibilities increase. Free time becomes harder to protect.

This is why early years matter.

You do not need perfection.

You need momentum.

Even modest progress made consistently can become meaningful over time.

Turn income growth into wealth growth

Higher income alone does not guarantee progress.

Many people earn more each year yet save little more.

Why?

Because lifestyle rises as fast as salary.

When income improves, use a rule:

Increase investing before increasing lifestyle.

For example:

- Raise SIP contributions after a salary increase
- Direct part of bonuses toward long-term goals
- Build emergency reserves faster
- Avoid permanent expenses based on temporary excitement

Learning that increases income becomes powerful when the extra income is invested wisely.

Avoid learning without direction

Not every course creates value.

Not every trend deserves attention.

Choose skills connected to:

- Your industry
- Your strengths
- Market demand
- Long-term usefulness
- Real earning potential

Random learning can waste time.

Focused learning builds leverage.

Ask yourself honestly:

- Have my skills grown as fast as my age?
- Has my income grown as fast as my effort?
- Will this skill help me become more useful, more effective, or better paid over time?

Those questions filter many distractions.

Growth does not require comparison

You do not need to compete with everyone. You only need to improve your own trajectory.

Better than last year is powerful.

One new skill each year can change a decade. One better financial decision after every raise can change retirement.

Quiet progress often looks small in the beginning. Then one day, it looks obvious.

The real advantage of prime years

Your younger years are valuable not because youth itself creates wealth.

They are valuable because:

- Learning may be easier
- Risk tolerance may be higher
- Time to recover is longer
- Time to compound is greater

That window should not be wasted entirely on consumption.

Use part of it to build earning power.

One day, responsibilities may grow and time may shrink.

What you quietly build in earlier years may one day protect you when life becomes heavier.

End-of-Chapter Summary

- In early years, skill growth can be one of your strongest wealth advantages
- Income often rises when your value rises
- Improving current work skills may be the simplest growth path
- Technology rewards adaptable learners
- Extra income creates wealth only when part of it is invested
- Focused learning is more powerful than random learning

One line to remember

Use your prime years to grow your value. Let that value grow your income, and let that income build your freedom.

CHAPTER TWENTY-NINE

Long-Term Wealth Habits — Final Advice for Staying the Course

Wealth is built quietly, not dramatically

Wealth is rarely built through a single brilliant decision. It grows through ordinary decisions repeated over many years.

There is rarely a defining moment or sudden breakthrough.

Most financially stable people did not win suddenly. They simply stayed consistent while others stopped, changed direction, or panicked.

This chapter is not about doing more. It is about staying steady.

If you've reached this chapter, you already have the patience most people never build.

The real enemy — inconsistency, not lack of knowledge

Most people already know enough to build wealth.

They know:

- Saving matters
- Investing early helps
- Compounding works

Yet results differ widely.

The gap is not knowledge. It is behaviour.

Wealth breaks when people:

- Stop investing during fear
- Chase returns after excitement
- Constantly change strategies
- Compare their journey with others

Inconsistency does more damage than a bad year in the market.

A simple plan followed for decades beats a brilliant plan followed for months.

The boring habits that actually create wealth

Long-term wealth habits are not exciting.

They are repetitive, dull, and often invisible.

The habits that matter most:

- Investing on schedule, not on mood
- Increasing SIPs gradually as income grows
- Reviewing finances once or twice a year — not daily
- Letting compounding work without interference

Wealth grows when money is allowed to stay invested.

Boredom in investing is not a flaw — it is a feature.

Staying invested during tough phases

Every long-term investor faces difficult periods.

Markets fall. Jobs change. Income pauses. Life interrupts plans. These phases are not exceptions. They are part of the journey.

The market does not reward bravery. It rewards patience.

Those who stay invested during uncertainty do not look smart at the time. They look disciplined later.

You do not need to predict recovery. You only need to remain present.

Detachment — letting money serve life, not control it

Money is a tool. Not an identity.

Net worth does not measure self-worth. Portfolio size does not define success.

Many financial mistakes come from emotional attachment:

- Buying homes too early
- Owning gadgets for status
- Paying for convenience without awareness

True financial maturity is knowing when enough is enough.

Money should support peace, flexibility, and dignity — not create pressure.

This is why everything you learned earlier — investing discipline, loan behaviour, lifestyle control, and habit building — ultimately points here: protecting consistency over decades.

Your system matters more than perfect returns

There is no single "best" financial plan.

The best plan is the one you can follow:

- During busy years
- During low motivation
- During stress
- During uncertainty

A slightly lower return with high discipline beats a higher return with frequent abandonment.

Simplicity protects consistency. Consistency protects compounding.

Wealth is personal.

Comparison quietly destroys it.

A lifetime view — wealth as a long partnership

Investing is not a phase of life. It evolves with life.

Early years focus on accumulation. Middle years focus on balance. Later years focus on stability and peace.

There is no finish line. Only adjustment.

Treat wealth as a long-term partner — not a short-term project.

When everything feels noisy, remember this

You do not need to react to every market movement. You do not need to optimise every decision. You do not need to act constantly.

Often, the most powerful financial move is simply doing nothing. Protect your habits. Protect your discipline. Protect your peace.

Let time do the work.

Final Reflection

You do not need perfection, brilliance, or speed.

You need patience, discipline, and enough honesty to stay consistent when progress feels slow.

Wealth is rarely built through dramatic moments.

It is built through calm decisions repeated over many years.

Avoid the major mistakes. Protect your time. Stay invested.

The rest often takes care of itself.

Final Line to Remember

Time builds wealth for those who stay patient long enough.

Note To The Reader

Your Next Step — A Simple Action Plan

You've understood the ideas. Now it's time to apply them — simply and consistently.

You don't need perfect knowledge to start. You need a clear first step — and the discipline to continue.

A simple plan to begin

1. Build your safety first

Create an emergency fund covering 3–6 months of expenses.
This protects your investments from being interrupted.

2. Start small, but start now

Begin with an amount you can continue comfortably.
Even ₹1,000–₹2,000 per month is enough.

3. Choose simplicity over complexity

Start with one or two mutual funds.
Avoid over-diversifying or chasing multiple options.

4. Automate your investments

Set up a monthly SIP.
Remove the need to decide every month.

5. Increase gradually

Whenever your income increases, increase your investment.
Growth in income should reflect in growth in investing.

6. Stay consistent through ups and downs

Do not stop when markets fall.
Consistency during uncertainty creates long-term results.

7. Review, don't react

Check your investments once or twice a year.
Avoid frequent changes based on short-term noise.

8. Protect your foundation

Keep insurance and emergency savings separate.
Do not mix long-term investments with short-term needs.

Progress does not come from intensity. It comes from consistency.

A final reminder:

You don't need to do everything perfectly.
You just need to avoid stopping.

And if you follow this...

If you follow this plan — not perfectly, but consistently — something begins to change.

Final Closing

One day, you will realise something quietly powerful:
Money is no longer a source of stress.
Not because you became rich overnight —
but because you became disciplined over time.
There was no single big decision. No perfect timing.
No moment where everything suddenly changed.
Just small, consistent actions — repeated over years.
You didn't interrupt what was working.
And slowly, without noise or excitement, things became stable.

Predictable. Under control.
And that is a form of freedom most people never reach.

www.ingramcontent.com/pod-product-compliance
Lightning Source LLC
LaVergne TN
LVHW100312210926
848480LV00003B/1102
* 9 7 9 8 9 0 5 6 0 6 6 6 3 *